Written by Isik Tlabar
Illustrated by Irem Kale
Edited by Isik Tlabar, Irem Kale and Aaron Le Conte
Cover design by İrem Kale, Aaron Le Conte, Isik Tlabar

Copyright © Isik Tlabar 2024

All rights reserved. No part of this publication may be reproduced or transmitted in any form or by any means, electronic or mechanical, including photocopying, recording, or by any information storage and retrieval system, without permission in writing from Isik Tlabar.

Single pages can be shared on social media when referencing the author Isik Tlabar @isiktlabar

www.isiktlabar.com

To my parents Ipek and Arif.

Thank you for loving me and teaching me how to be a good hearted human being.

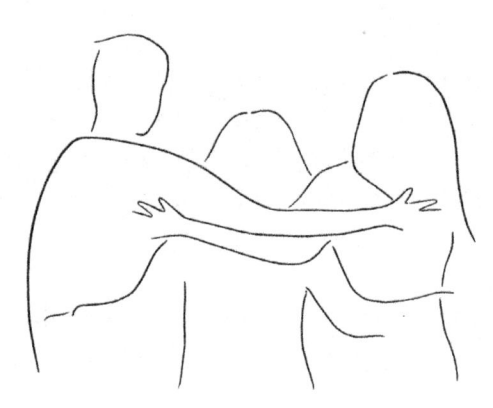

140 THINGS
I WISH I KNEW
WHEN I WAS 14

A Book for Teen Girls to Believe In Themselves and Follow Their Dreams

IŞIK TLABAR

CONTENTS

ACKNOWLEDGEMENTS	9
WHY 14?	11
HOW DID THIS BOOK COME ABOUT?	13
HOW TO READ THIS BOOK?	15
A FEW HEADS UP	16
FRIENDS	18
Part 1 - Your Friends	19
Part 2 - Making Friends	21
Part 3 - See Yourself in Others	23
Part 4 - Respect & Love	25
Part 5 - Ask Support From Your Friends	29
Part 6 - Be Interesting to Others	31
Part 7 - You Can Be Kind and Have Boundaries	33
Part 8 - You Can Change Your Mind	32
Part 9 - Own Your No	34
Part 10 - Say Sorry	35
Part 11 - Your Friends Will Change	37
Part 12 - Let Go of Friends	39
Part 13 - Love Your Own Company	41
SCHOOL	48
Part 14 - Belonging	49
Part 15 - Don't Try To Fit In	51
Part 16 - Starting a New School	53
Part 17 - Let Go of the Bullies	56
Part 18 - True Power	57

Part 19 - Don't Gossip   59
Part 20 - Don't Take Things Personally   61
Part 21 - Stressing at School   63
Part 22 - School Work   65
Part 23 - Test Anxiety   67

PARENTS   74

Part 24 - The First Relationship You Have   75
Part 25 - Accept Parents As They Are   77
Part 26 - Parents Are Also Humans   79
Part 27 - Neglectful Parents   81
Part 28 - Parents Divorcing   83
Part 29 - Middle Child   85
Part 30 - Strict Parents   87
Part 31 - Privacy at Home   89
Part 32 - Dad Seeing You As Failure   91
Part 33 - Mum Commenting on Your Appearance   93
Part 34 - Wanting Mum To Be Different   97
Part 35 - Being Triggered By Your Parents   99
Part 36 - Connect With Your Inner Child   101
Part 37 - Write a Letter to Your Parents   103
Part 38 - Sharing Your Dreams With Your Parents   105
Part 39 - Parental Wounds   109
Part 40 - Forgive Your Parents   113

RELATIONSHIPS   124

Part 41 - Choose The Love You Want   125
Part 42 - Don't Repeat the Past   127
Part 43 - Is Your Crush Real?   129
Part 44 - Share Your Feelings With Your Crush   131

Part 45 - Be Brave In Love   133
Part 46 - Don't Overstretch Your Heart   135
Part 47 - Don't Look To Be Saved   137
Part 48 - Being Chosen by a Boy   139
Part 49 - Rejection   141
Part 50 - Your Worth is Not About Your Looks   143
Part 51 - Speak Your Truth   145
Part 52 - Getting Over Someone   147
Part 53 - Conscious Uncoupling   152

EMOTIONS   164

Part 54 - What Are Emotions?   165
Part 55 - Process Your Emotions   167
Part 56 - You're Allowed To Feel   169
Part 57 - Let Go Of Emotions   171
Part 58 - Fear   174
Part 59 - Jealousy   175
Part 60 - Negative Thoughts   177
Part 61 - Share Feelings   179
Part 62 - You're Worthy   181
Part 63 - Feeling Lonely   183
Part 64 - Be Kind To Yourself   185
Part 65 - Feedback   187
Part 66 - Learn From Past Mistakes   189
Part 67 - You're Loved   191
Part 68 - You're Not Too Much   193
Part 69 - Love Yourself In Loneliness   195
Part 70 - Trust People   197
Part 71 - This Will Pass   199

SELF CARE   204

Part 72 - Self-Care Is Important   205
Part 73 - Learn To Look After Yourself   207
Part 74 - Replace Addictions With Connections   209
Part 75 - Make Your Bed   211
Part 76 - Drink Water   213
Part 77 - Tidy Room   215
Part 78 - Declutter   217
Part 79 - Go To Bed Early   219
Part 80 - Allow Yourself To Rest   222
Part 81 - Nourish Yourself   223
Part 82 - Nature   225
Part 83 - Dance it Out   227
Part 84 - Shake Your Body   229
Part 85 - Morning Pages   231
Part 86 - Let Go Of Emotions   233
Part 87 - Little Book of Magic   235
Part 88 - Stay In Your Own Energy   237

BE YOURSELF   240

Part 89 - Be Yourself   241
Part 90 - Different Parts   243
Part 91 - Who You Are   245
Part 92 - You're Unique   247
Part 93 - Create Your Own Style   249
Part 94 - Focus On Your Surroundings   251
Part 95 - You Don't Have To Be Perfect   253
Part 96 - Your Worth Is Not Based On What You Do   255
Part 97 - Share Yourself   257
Part 98 - Take Up Space   259

Part 99 - Confidence	261
Part 100 - You Know	263
Part 101 - Make Your Own Choices	265
Part 102 - We're All Equal	267
Part 103 - Ask For Help	269
Part 104 - Allow Change	271
Part 105 - Put Yourself In The Right Environment	273
Part 106 - You Will Become	275
Part 107 - Allow Yourself To Evolve	277

DREAMS 286

Part 108 - Your Dreams Are Powerful	287
Part 109 - Ego vs Soul	289
Part 110 - Own Your Dreams	291
Part 111 - Discover Your Dreams	293
Part 112 - Listen To Your Intuition	295
Part 113 - Connect To The Magic Of Life	297
Part 114 - Connect With Your Truth	301
Part 115 - Egoic And True Vision	304
Part 116 - Trust Yourself	307
Part 117 - You Can Do Anything	309
Part 118 - Conscious Creation	311
Part 119 - Masculine And Feminine In Creation	314
Part 120 - Trust Your Timing	317
Part 121 - Follow Your Dream	319
Part 122 - Write Your Dreams	321
Part 123 - Believe In Your Dreams	327
Part 124 - Receive Guidance From Your Higher Self	330
Part 125 - One Step At A Time	332
Part 126 - Feel Inspired By Others	333
Part 127 - Fear Of Failure	335

Part 128 - You're Not Too Young	337
Part 129 - Decide And Act	339
Part 130 - Do Your Best	341
Part 131 - Keep Going Towards Your Dreams	343
WOMANHOOD	**352**
Part 132 - You're Becoming A Woman	353
Part 133 - Your Body Is A Miracle	355
Part 134 - Love Your Body	357
Part 135 - You're Beautiful	360
Part 136 - Make-Up	363
Part 137 - Sisterhood	365
Part 138 - Periods	367
Part 139 - Enjoy Your Attractions	371
Part 140 - Don't Rush Into Sex	373
NOW WHAT?	381
WHAT WAS I LIKE WHEN I WAS 14?	383
HOW DID I BECOME WHO I AM NOW?	385
WHAT I STUDIED & WHAT I DO NOW	387
BOOKS	389
ABOUT THE AUTHOR	391
ABOUT THE ILLUSTRATOR	392

ACKNOWLEDGEMENTS

This book was a labour of love. Love is poured into all of its corners. I didn't do this alone.

I'd like to thank a few people who made a real impact in the creation of it.

Mum - I love you. Thank you for always being there for me. Thank you for everything you've taught me, especially going after what I want and for showing me that everything is possible. Your achievements in life inspired me to go after my dreams. Your big heart inspires and impacts so many people and I'm infinitely grateful for your unconditional support, love and wisdom.

14 year old me - We did it! We've written a book together. I got to know you so much better through this process and I think you're amazing. I love you. And I'm so proud of you.

TikTok Teens - This book wouldn't be possible without you. You made this project what it is. Your questions informed the chapters. Thank you for all of your comments and shares. It meant the world to me to see so many of you applying the tips. Thank you for your openness, vulnerability and courage. You have touched my heart deeply.

Irem - I couldn't have asked for a better collaborator. You poured so much love, care, devotion and hard work into this. Thank you for your wholehearted dedication and "all in" attitude throughout this journey. Your capacity to naturally tune in to the energy and my vision is something I am so grateful for. Your incredible illustrations capture the essence of each chapter and thank you also for helping with the editing. Thank you for everything; we truly did it together and I appreciate you more than words can express.

Aaron - You're the greatest friend that anyone could ask for. You've been there for me countless times, patiently continuing to remind me of the essence of this book, what I had set out to do when I had lost touch with it. Thank you for all your suggestions over the last three years in creating this. I am forever grateful for your friendship, love and support.

Roisin - Thank you for your initial editing, professional advice and your encouragement in the potential of this project.

Daisy, Barbara, Catalina, Irem, Aaron - Thank you for proofreading, editing and giving your valuable time and much appreciated feedback.

Lauren, Glenn, Tom, Charlie, Rodrigo, Nathalie, Binta, Dan, Gute, Natalie, Celynn, Duke, Grant, Seani, Steve, Neil, Raffa, Alice, Elise, Lucia, Steph, Neo, Gary, Elliott, Joanna, Claire, Adam, Will, Ali, Yasmeen, Hamed, Leela, Maryam, Sorrel, Chloe, Gina, Carol, Lottie, Eva, Debora, Todd, Avanti, Elaine, Sherin, Fiona, Alexey, Kat, Ryan, William, Christian, Pandora, Amanda, Maya, Fatih, Ilgin, Seza, Zeynep, Ridvan, Kubra, Aysun, Burak, Oya, Yasemin, Yeliz, Yunus, Melahat, Melis, Bahadir, Murat, Carina, Can, Zuhal, Acar, Hazel, Seynan, Dilek, Suheyla, Figen, Inci, Deniz, Bora, Evren, Songul, Osman, Berk, Cansel, clients and friends - Thank you for believing in me and in this book. Your words, love, support, advice and insights meant a lot.

Thank you to everyone who supported me in the creation of this book. I love you.

I hope you enjoy it!

WHY 14?

14 is the age when you're not a child anymore.

You're not quite an adult yet either.

It's that weird in-between phase.

It's when a caterpillar is not a caterpillar anymore, nor is it a butterfly quite yet.

Instead a mushy thing that is about to become a butterfly.

It can feel scary.

You might feel lost, lonely or sad.

You're becoming a teenager.

You might be beginning a new school.

So I thought, these were the things I wish I knew when I was 14. However you can be 13, 15, 16 or any age to read this guide.

This is the book I wish I had read when I was 14.

This is the book I wish I had to guide me on how to go about "life".

I'm writing this book as a gift to my inner 14 year old and to all the teen girls out there.

HOW DID THIS BOOK COME ABOUT?

This book started as a Tiktok series towards the end of 2020.

I wanted to share what I wish I'd known, when I was younger, in a practical and simple way.

I remember the first video was about trusting yourself.

As I made the videos, the response was amazing.

The videos started to reach many people.

I saw how needed this was.

Teenagers on TikTok started to share their experiences and ask questions.

Half of this book was created from those questions.

They applied the tips, came back and shared how it went.

At some point, I started ending the videos with "You're amazing in every way".

It just came out.

The chapters came from the topics that it seems that most teens struggle with.

I definitely struggled with those and my friends did too.

I divided the book into 9 chapters:

Friends	Relationships	Be Yourself
School	Emotions	Dreams
Parents	Self-Care	Womanhood

At the end of each chapter, I kept some of the most popular questions and answers from the series.

After a lot of hard work of 3 years in the making, here is the final book.

I have loved creating this book.

My wish is that it empowers you to be yourself, to trust yourself and to follow your dreams.

May it give you inner peace.

May it help you believe in yourself.

May it give you hope about your future.

May it make you see that you're amazing in every way.

HOW TO READ THIS BOOK?

You can read this book however you like.

You can start from the beginning and read until the end.

When you feel lost and looking for an answer, you can open up a page and read that.

It's a guide to support you.

To help you be a human.

And to remind you of who you are.

A FEW HEADS UP

1. Take what you need, leave the rest:

You might not agree with everything in this book.

That's ok.

If something doesn't resonate with you, let it go.

And keep reading.

2. Make the wording your own:

I wrote this book with teen girls in mind.

I'm using the word "girl" a lot.

But if you happen to be a male, woman, non-binary, adult, or whoever you are, make the wording your own.

If I said something wrong, don't take it personally :)

Translate it into your voice so it speaks to you.

FRIENDS

Part 1 - Your Friends

Friends are like the family we choose.

They can be as close to us as we want them to be.

Not all of your friends are your closest friends.

With some, you go deep and you can talk for hours.

With some, maybe you see each other once in 6 months and you don't talk very deeply.

Not every friend will hold your heart like your closest ones.

A good friend of mine gave me an analogy about this:

You're like the sun of your own solar system.

You have the planets around you.

They're your friends.

Not all of your friends are Mercuries.

Some can be Plutos.

Yet they're still in your solar system.

A friend can be a Pluto friend.

But you might be trying to keep them close like a Mercury friend.

Let the energy between you two naturally inform your friend's position in your solar system.

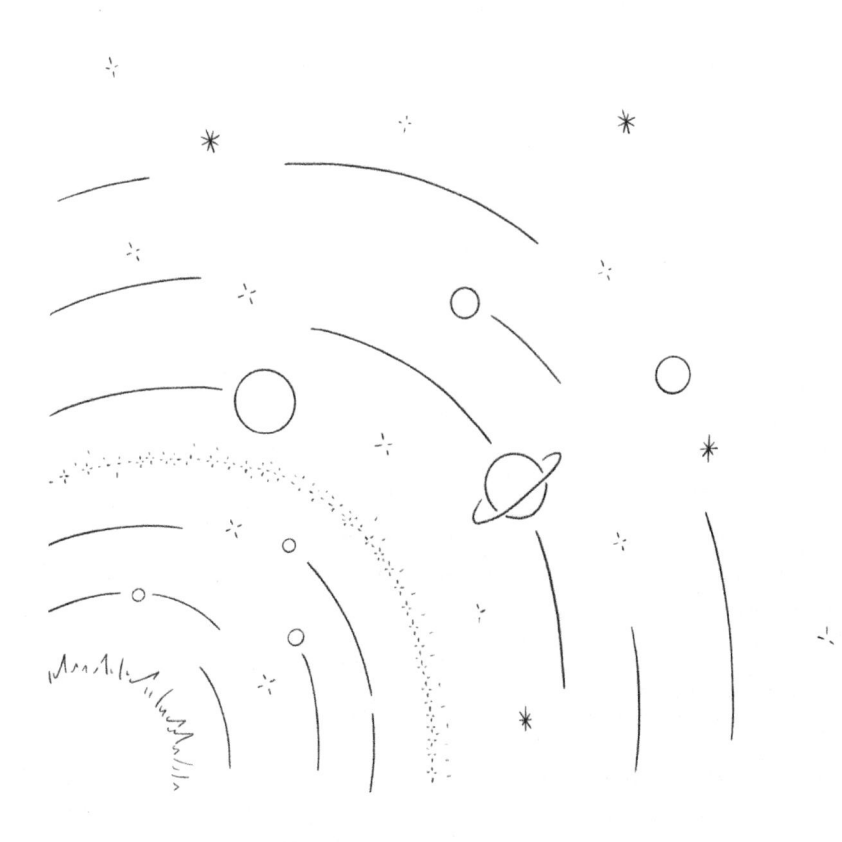

You're amazing in every way :)

Part 2 - Making Friends

Becoming interested in people is the best way of making friends.

Instead of sharing about yourself, ask them,

"What are your dreams?"

"What do you like?"

People naturally light up when they talk about something they love.

Listen to them.

Give them your full presence.

Ask them questions.

If there's common interests between you, share that.

Next time you see them, make a reference to your previous conversation and ask them,

"Hey how did X go?"

They will feel valued and seen.

If you want people to be interested in you, be interested in them.

Talk to them.

You can go up to someone and give them a compliment.

People love receiving compliments.

You can compliment their hair, what they're wearing etc.

Otherwise it might feel like you're always waiting for someone to show interest in you.

Go out and chat.

You're amazing in every way :)

Part 3 - See Yourself in Others

You have within you what you see in others.

For example, if you recognise how open and loving someone is, you have the same quality inside of you as well.

The qualities you admire in others, you might not have fully embodied them within yourself yet.

That's ok, you can see this as an opportunity to express these qualities more.

If you ever feel jealous of someone, know that the qualities you are jealous of, are inside of you already.

The more you see how open someone is, allow that openness to expand inside of you.

The more you see how loving someone is, allow that love to expand inside of you.

The more you see how free someone is, allow that freedom to expand inside of you.

You're amazing in every way :)

Part 4 - Respect & Love

Choose to be with people who respect and love you.

Don't spend too much time and energy on trying to get someone's love.

You already deserve that love.

You're already worthy and loved, as you are.

Those who love you, will make it clear to you that they do.

They won't leave you questioning.

Be with people who make you feel at ease when you're with them.

You're amazing in every way :)

Part 5 - Ask Support From Your Friends

When you feel lonely or need support, have a friend you can reach out to.

Ask if you can reach out to them when you're feeling low.

If they say yes, you can tell them what you need to hear in those times.

It can be something like:

"Hey, can I reach out to you when I feel lonely? Can you tell me that I'm not alone and I'm loved?"

Whatever you need to hear.

I do this with one or two of my friends.

Remember that you can ask for support from your friends.

You can also offer them the same.

So that you've got each other's back.

You're amazing in every way :)

Part 6 - Be Interesting to Others

If you want to be interesting to others, do what brings you joy.

Do what you love.

Maybe it's listening to music, painting or writing.

Focus on what you enjoy doing creatively.

Because when you do that, you're naturally radiant, happy and more attractive to others.

You're naturally in a higher energy.

Look at someone who's really cool.

They're probably doing what they love.

When you do what you love, it really changes your energy.

When you give yourself what you want, you're attractive to others.

When you're in that place of really enjoying what you're doing, that energy will go out.

And you're going to attract your new friends.

I love dancing.

I met some of my best friends on the dance floor.

Because I was doing what brought me joy.

They were there doing what brought them joy too.

We spoke the same language.

We had similar passions.

You can meet like minded people by following your passion.

You're amazing in every way :)

Part 7 - You Can Be Kind and Have Boundaries

Boundaries are where you end and someone else begins.

When you say "no" to someone, you're saying "yes" to yourself.

They're the limits you choose. They can create more safety for you.

If someone is treating you in a disrespectful way, you can say:

"That's not ok. You can't treat me that way."

If they're making fun of you, say it again:

"That's not ok. You can't treat me that way."

Stay in your power and hold your ground. Don't worry about making them feel uncomfortable.

You deserve to be treated with love, respect and kindness.

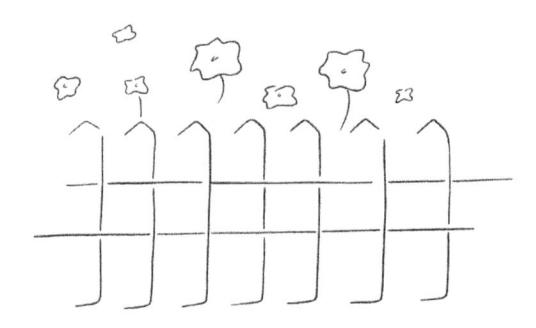

You're amazing in every way :)

Part 8 - You Can Change Your Mind

You can say "yes" to your friend.

Then change your mind to a "no".

You're allowed to change your mind.

Let your friends know your truth.

This might upset them and that's ok.

You can say, "I'm really sorry."

Don't abandon yourself to please others.

Don't compromise to fit in.

You're amazing in every way :)

Part 9 - Own Your No

You can say "no" to people.

When someone asks you to do something and it doesn't feel true to do it, don't do it.

You can say:

"I appreciate you asking me, but I'm not able to do that right now."

Or you can offer another option:

"I won't be able to do it now. How about later today or tomorrow?"

Only offer the alternative if you feel like offering it.

You don't have to explain your "no", if you don't want to.

It's a "no".

You're amazing in every way :)

Part 10 - Say Sorry

Making mistakes is the most human thing.

It's not about trying to not make mistakes.

It's about how you repair from the mistake or the hurt.

If you were mean to someone at school, here's how you can apologise:

Firstly, say that you're sorry.

Really own what you did and come from your heart.

"Hey Sarah, I want to apologise for what I did. I'm really sorry that I was mean to you."

Secondly, tell them the effect your actions had on them.

Show them that you understand how painful it was for them.

"I can see how much it upset you and how much it affected you."

Thirdly, tell them what you're going to do differently, now so that it doesn't happen again.

"I won't do that again in the future."

You can end with:

"Will you forgive me?"

The best is saying this in-person, if not have a call, send a voicenote or write it out.

Well done for apologising.

We're all humans, we all make mistakes.

It's not about not making mistakes, but it's how we rectify these mistakes that shows our integrity and heart.

You're amazing in every way :)

Part 11 - Your Friends Will Change

Throughout your life, some friends will stay.

Some friends will come and go.

And that's just life.

We sometimes walk alongside each other until we don't.

It might hurt after a friendship is over, but know that you will make new friends.

That space will be filled with new friendships.

Or whatever you want to fill it with.

If someone broke your trust, know that the past is over.

It doesn't have to be repeated.

You can make a new choice now.

Don't let the negativity of the past impact your future.

Don't carry it into future relationships.

Start from ground zero and let it build.

If they have broken your trust, take this into consideration for your future interactions with them.

Give them a chance to regain your trust, if you are willing to do that.

Don't focus on how hurt you were in the past.

Focus on how different you'd like things to be now.

Put your attention onto that.

You're going to create great friendships.

You're amazing in every way :)

Part 12 - Let Go of Friends

Your friends will change over the years.

Losing a friend can feel like a breakup.

It might feel like your world is ending.

But it gets better.

Trust me.

If you don't feel appreciated, celebrated and honoured for who you truly are, you can move away from a friendship.

If there's guilt in that, let the guilt go.

Follow your truth.

Do what feels right for you.

If you see that the person has moved on already, know that we never know what's going on for someone else.

People deal with it in different ways.

Some people deal with the pain straight away.

Some people seem like they moved on, but it can be a facade.

You don't know the whole story.

Don't assume.

Don't look back.

There will be many more friends to come.

Go and create new friendships.

You're amazing in every way :)

Part 13 - Love Your Own Company

It's really important to learn to love spending time with yourself.

This way you get to know yourself better.

You get to find out what you like.

What you don't like.

What you care about.

What you're passionate about.

Then, when you choose to hang out with someone, it's a choice and not a need.

Because you're good on your own already.

When you're with yourself, fill your time with things that you enjoy doing.

Imagine you're going on a date with yourself.

How would you treat yourself?

What would you do?

Follow that.

You're amazing in every way :)

Q&A 1

"Hi <3 Can you help me with how to deal with not getting invited? My friends just went out without me and it made me really sad.."

I'm so sorry this happened.

It's ok to feel that sadness.

Feel it and honour it.

Know that it doesn't mean anything about you.

It doesn't mean you're not loveable or you're not fun to be around.

There's no meaning. Nothing is personal.

All that happened was that you weren't invited. That's it.
Let it go.

Focus on friends who do celebrate you, who do cherish, love and include you.

You're amazing in every way :)

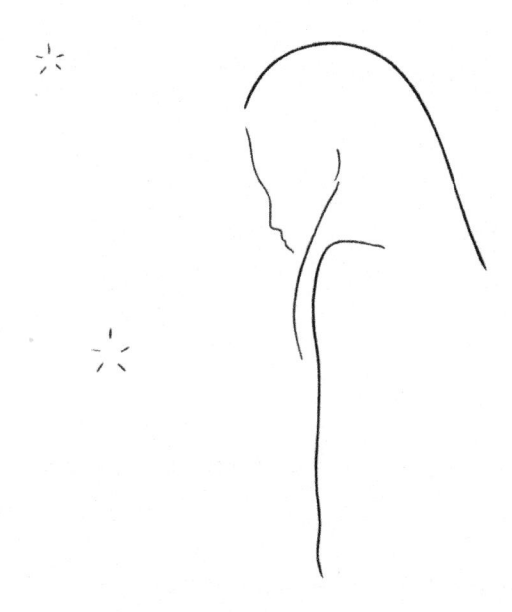

Q&A 2

"How do you get your boyfriend's mum to like you? Or how do you get a good relationship with her? I love your content! It helps me a lot :)"

First off, you can't get everyone to like you and that's ok.

But there are two things you can do.

Firstly, be interested in her.

Ask her questions.

Listen.

Show her you're listening.

Make her feel like she's the most amazing person on the planet at that moment.

Be fascinated by this person in front of you.

You will never meet any other person like her again.

You can also give her a compliment.

Secondly, and most importantly, be yourself!

Don't be who you think you should be for someone to like you.

Be who you are.

And if they don't like you, that's ok.

It's their loss.

Someone else will see you and love you for who you are.

And if your boyfriend's mum is seeing her son happy with you, she probably already likes you.

You're amazing in every way :)

SCHOOL

Part 14 - Belonging

We first experience the feeling of belonging in our family.

This feeling of belonging extends into the school we go to.

Then, it carries on into creating our own life and feeling our place in the world.

If you feel like you don't belong in your school, that's ok.

You might feel like you don't know your place in the world.

Or feel no one in your school understands you.

It's ok to feel that way.

This feeling will pass and you won't feel this way forever.

You're amazing in every way :)

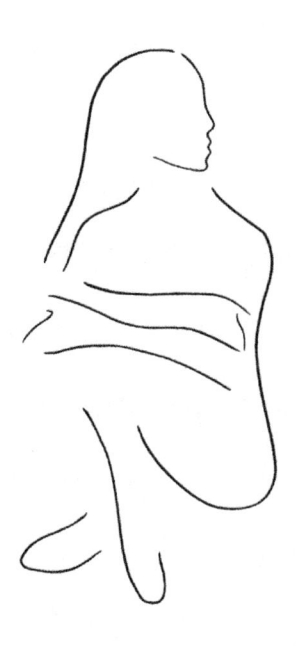

Part 15 - Don't Try To Fit In

In every school, there are friendship groups.

Just like in society.

There are the popular ones.

The creative ones.

The sporty ones.

The nerdy ones and more.

You don't have to make yourself smaller to fit into any group.

You don't even have to be in any group.

Never abandon yourself in order to be loved.

Be yourself authentically.

You're amazing in every way :)

Part 16 - Starting a New School

Starting a new school can be both daunting and exciting.

It could also be an opportunity to let go of your past school experience and create a new beginning.

A clean slate where you get to start all over.

If you have just started a new school, here are three tips to make the most out of a new school:

1. Decide who you want to be

No one knows you in this school.

No one has any idea who you are, what you're about and what your past is.

Ask yourself:

"Who would I like to be?"

"How would I like to be?"

Bring more of that outside.

If you're someone who is more likely to be shy, and you want to be more social, you can choose to be more outgoing and talk to people.

Don't abandon your true nature.

And at the same time, you can always reinvent yourself.

2. See it as your new playground

You're starting a new adventure.

Everything's new.

Anything is possible.

This new school is your playground.

Whenever there's an opportunity to join something you love or to collaborate, jump into that.

Say "yes" first.

Think about how to do it later.

It might create magic.

You'll never know.

3. Don't sweat the small stuff

If there are people you don't like, don't worry about them.

You're probably not going to be seeing them ever again in 4-5 years.

So let them go.

You're amazing in every way :)

Part 17 - Let Go of the Bullies

Bullies bully because they have often been bullied.

They may have been bullied earlier in their lives or in other areas of their lives.

Or they learnt to be that way in order to look powerful.

So no one messes with them.

But inside, they often feel weak, fragile and insecure.

When a bully tries to put you down, don't accept what they say.

Don't take what they're saying to heart.

Tell them, "You can't talk to me this way."

And hold your ground.

You're amazing in every way :)

hold your heart

Part 18 - True Power

At one point in our lives, we might choose to overpower others to feel powerful and in charge.

Know that you're powerful as you are.

There is power in your softness, sensitivity and vulnerability.

This is true power.

Would you like to be treated in the way you're treating this person in front of you?

Treat others how you'd like to be treated.

And you'll receive ten folds of that.

You're amazing in every way :)

softness, sensibility and vulnerability

this is true power

Part 19 - Don't Gossip

Gossip is an uncreative way of connecting with people.

It's a way to pull yourself up by putting others down.

Don't bond with people over gossip.

You can bond with people talking about what you love and what your passions are.

It's way more inspiring and uplifting.

And if people are gossiping about you, let them.

You're probably not going to be speaking to these people in a few years time anyway.

People who truly know your authentic self won't be affected by such gossip.

So don't worry about what they say.

You're amazing in every way :)

Part 20 - Don't Take Things Personally

Don't take things personally.

We tend to make how people behave towards us, mean something about us.

If someone is being mean to you, it often doesn't mean anything about you.

You don't know their whole story.

Maybe they just had a bad day.

Maybe they feel insecure about themselves.

Or maybe they feel lonely.

Just because you're on the receiving end, doesn't make what they say true.

For example, it might make you feel like you're a bad person.

In truth, you're not.

How people treat you says more about them than it does about you.

You're amazing in every way :)

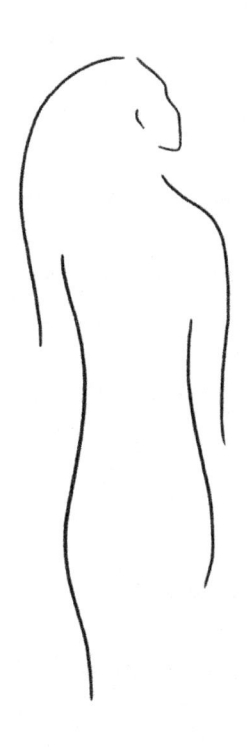

Part 21 - Stressing at School

Experiencing stress at school is very natural.

There's a lot of workload and a lot to do.

And very little time to do it all.

What you can do is, divide the workload into smaller tasks.

This will make it feel more manageable.

Look at what you need to do monthly, weekly and daily.

Every time you finish a task, give yourself something to celebrate.

It can be as easy as marking it done with a colourful pen on your schedule.

Doing a little dance.

Giving yourself a pat on the back.

See it like you're walking up a staircase.

If you look at the whole staircase, it's going to look like there are a lot of steps.

It could feel overwhelming.

But if you know that's the staircase you're walking up, then all you need to focus on is the next step.

Then the next step..

Then the next step...

And the next.

Then you're going to find yourself at the end of the staircase.

So take it one step at a time.

See the whole picture and focus on what you need to do next.

You're amazing in every way :)

Part 22 - School Work

You might be struggling to do school work.

Sometimes it's hard to find the motivation.

Because not all these subjects might interest you.

What you can do is link the school work to something you care about.

Something like this:

"If I do my school work, I'll have time to draw, paint, write, dance, daydream.."

You'll be free and you'll have way more space in your mind to do what you love.

When you graduate, you'll have the freedom to do whatever you want.

You've got this!

You're amazing in every way :)

Part 23 - Test Anxiety

It's totally ok to have test anxiety.

I had it as well.

When I was in high school, I really didn't enjoy them.

Know that this is temporary.

How good you are in life is not going to be measured with how good you are at tests in school.

Acknowledge how you feel:

"Ok, I feel anxious about the test."

Tell yourself:

"I can do this."

You can feel nervous about something and still do well.

Instead of worrying about not doing well, put your focus into doing well.

Give it your 100%.

No matter what, at least you know you gave it your all.

You're amazing in every way :)

Q&A 1

"I have math anxiety. I get so worried about math, then I get so much things wrong on the test"

It's totally ok to feel anxious.

There's nothing wrong with it.

But there are things you can do to help with it.

Here's a quick breathing exercise you can do before the test.

Breathe in through your nose for 4.

1.. 2.. 3.. 4

And then exhale from the nose for 6.

1.. 2.. 3.. 4.. 5.. 6

Make sure to exhale longer than you inhale.

This allows you to calm down and be more present.

Do this for five minutes before the test.

Then visualise yourself doing amazing at the test.

See yourself absolutely smashing and nailing it.

Go into the test focusing on that end result.

Sometimes you might think the test didn't go well, but you get a good result.

Sometimes you might think it went well, but you don't get a result that reflects that.

That's ok, it happens.

Getting a bad test result isn't a reflection of your worth.

It's just information about the level of knowledge you have on this topic.

So give your 100% and let the rest go.

Good luck! You got this.

You're amazing in every way :)

Q&A 2

"Hi, do grades matter in life? And what if you don't have the perfect grades? Pls answer I've been so worried about this"

There might be a lot of pressure on you right now to get good grades.

Grades help you access the next level in life.

Either to go to university or pursue a career for example.

I sucked at math.

I sucked at many science related subjects.

It just didn't come naturally to me.

I still put in the hard work to do well in those subjects.

Even though I didn't enjoy them, I did well which allowed me to go into university to study architecture in the UK.

That was the beginning of following my dreams.

After graduating, I created my own business to help people.

Getting good grades opened up the door to live in the UK, so I can start to create a new life there.

The more time you put into studying, the less worried you'll be about your abilities.

The more you practise something, the more confident you'll feel about it.

Use the worry to put in the hard work and you'll see the results.

It's ok if you don't have the perfect grades, just focus on doing your best.

You're amazing in every way :)

PARENTS

Part 24 - The First Relationship You Have

Your parents are the first two people you meet in life.

Your relationship with your parents is the first relationship you have.

They will give you the blueprint of men and women.

Every relationship you have with others, will reflect the one you have with them.

With women, you'll reflect the relationship you have with your mother.

Or whoever represented the feminine for you.

With men, you'll reflect the relationship you have with your father.

Or whoever represented the masculine for you.

As a starting point at least.

They are two of the most important relationships in your life.

When you heal this, you also heal all the other relationships.

At times you might experience difficulties, conflicts and arguments with them.

This is where you also get to discover yourself.

Be kind to yourself with the relationship you have with your parents.

You're amazing in every way :)

Part 25 - Accept Parents As They Are

You might be feeling disappointed by your parents.

They might make you feel sad, angry or disappointed.

I know this is hard.

But try to accept them as they are.

Let go of expectations of how your parents should show up.

Stop wanting your parents to be how you want them to be.

This will only cause more suffering.

Suffering comes from wanting others to be how you want them to be.

They're a whole different generation.

They experience the world differently.

You are the next generation in the family.

You might experience the world differently to them.

It's natural.

So let go of all the expectations and be yourself.

You're amazing in every way :)

Part 26 - Parents Are Also Humans

Being a parent is the hardest job on the planet.

Parents are also humans.

Parental love is the most vulnerable love.

It's a constant lesson in letting go.

When you stop being a toddler and become a child, they let you go.

When you leave home for school or university, they let go.

And many more moments.

It's like wearing your heart on your sleeve as you, their child, goes out into the world.

It's like letting a piece of your heart go.

They also really don't know what they're doing.

No one taught them how to do this.

They don't know how to be a parent until they become one.

You are allowed to feel how you're feeling about them.

You're so right.

And also try to see the situation from their perspective.

Maybe they made mistakes.

Just like you have made mistakes.

They're not perfect.

It's very common that our parents feel guilt for what they've done or didn't do.

They might cherish you too much or too little.

Try to see them through the eyes of empathy.

Notice what you see.

You're amazing in every way :)

Part 27 - Neglectful Parents

Experiencing neglect in any way is painful.

This can be even more painful when it comes from the very people that brought you into this world.

It might make you feel you're unlovable.

You're too much.

Or there's something wrong with you.

You might feel,

"If they didn't love me, who will?"

None of these stories are true.

The truth might have been that they were too busy working, trying to make a living to look after you.

Or that they didn't have the emotional capacity to meet your needs.

Because they didn't get this modelled for them either.

Your experience of family isn't limited to your initial family.

If you want to create your own family, you can create a loving, supportive, warm and connected atmosphere in your own way.

There's always hope.

If that's what your heart wants, you can have that.

You're amazing in every way :)

Part 28 - Parents Divorcing

Your parents might be going through a divorce.

Know that, it's not your fault.

It has nothing to do with you.

It doesn't mean you were not good enough for them.

It doesn't mean that they didn't love you.

You did nothing wrong.

It just didn't work out between your parents.

And it's not your job to fix it either.

Your parents love you.

They're always going to love you.

No matter what happens between them.

You're amazing in every way :)

Part 29 - Middle Child

When you're a middle child, sometimes you might feel left out.

You might feel your feelings or needs don't matter.

Know that your parents love you.

Sometimes they don't have the capacity, time or the energy to express that.

It doesn't mean they don't love you.

It doesn't mean your feelings don't matter.

You matter.

Your feelings matter.

And you're so loved.

The way someone treats you doesn't make you more or less lovable.

You're loveable as you are.

Keep expressing your feelings and know that you're so loved.

You're amazing in every way :)

Part 30 - Strict Parents

I know it's hard to have strict parents.

You might feel like you're not being heard.

You're not being listened to.

You're not being acknowledged for who you are or what you want.

It can feel frustrating to have your parents have the final say.

It can feel like you don't have a say in it leaving you feeling powerless.

That can feel unfair.

Your parents probably had strict parents as well.

They're only doing the parenting they know how to do.

They might believe control is the way to discipline and to raise a child.

Know that this isn't going to last forever.

When you're older, you can live however you want to live.

So set yourself free.

You're amazing in every way :)

Part 31 - Privacy at Home

At home, you might not have much personal space right now.

You might be worried that your parents are going to walk in on you.

You might not have a lock.

And you might be feeling anxious about not having privacy.

I completely feel and understand you.

It's hard. It sucks.

But one day you're going to have your own room.

Your own home.

You're going to be able to do whatever you want.

This will pass.

It's not always going to be like this forever.

In a few years time, when you're living in your own house, you're going to look back at yourself today.

You will smile to the version of you today and say,

"We made it."

You're amazing in every way :)

Part 32 - Dad Seeing You As Failure

You're not a failure.

Maybe your dad sees you as a failure.

If this is the case, there might be a part in him that sees himself as a failure too.

It might be how he feels about himself.

Or what his dad told him.

He had an expectation of you which didn't happen.

The expectation came from him, not you.

So it has nothing to do with you.

It's not personal.

Also ask yourself this:

"Is my measure of success the same as your dad's?"

If not, it's just how he sees success.

Maybe your dad values security.

And you value freedom.

So keep being you.

Let your dad have his own opinion.

It doesn't matter, if it doesn't align with yours.

This is your life.

You get to decide what success is for you.

Follow that.

You're amazing in every way :)

Part 33 - Mum Commenting on Your Appearance

You might have a mum that constantly criticises everything about you.

When people feel a certain way about themselves, they tend to project it onto others.

Projection means attributing how you feel about yourself towards others.

And you might be the "others" in this situation.

If your mum calls you hurtful words like,

"You're ugly"

"You're worthless"

She might be saying things she feels about herself.

Or she believes this is what she needs to say as a mum.

Maybe her own mum called her these words too.

Maybe her own mum criticised her and she carried on doing that.

I know it's hard and it sucks.

Try not to pay attention to it.

Every time your mum tells you,

"You're worthless"

You tell yourself,

"I'm worthy of love".

Every time she tells you,

"You're useless"

You tell yourself,

"I have a lot to offer"

Every time she insults you or is mean to you, remind yourself,

"This is how she treats herself."

This is probably her inner critic speaking to her inner child.

You can also tell her,

"Mum, that's not ok that you're calling me ugly. Please don't call me that again."

This is a boundary you set.

If she laughs, just repeat what you said.

It's healthy to have boundaries with your mum.

Sometimes it takes a long time to build a boundary.

Every time you express your boundary, the boundary gets stronger.

So every time she says hurtful words, imagine it's washing over you.

Just like water.

Flowing away.

Then close your eyes, place your hand on your heart and tell yourself,

"I'm so loved. I'm whole and complete."

Give yourself a hug and tell yourself,

"I'm beautiful inside and out."

Because that's the truth.

You're amazing in every way :)

Part 34 - Wanting Mum To Be Different

Sometimes we wish our mums were different.

Sometimes we wish they had loved us in the way we actually wanted to be loved.

Sometimes we want them to be softer, kinder and more loving.

But nearly every time, the mum we have is the perfect mum for us.

Even if it may be hard at times, there may be a lesson there.

They're the mum we needed to have to be who we are today.

You're amazing in every way :)

Part 35 - Being Triggered By Your Parents

Spending time with your parents can be challenging.

Ram Daas said,

"If you think you're enlightened, go spend a week with your family."

Here's what you can do if you're interacting with a family member you find challenging:

Breathe.

Take deep breaths throughout your time with them.

As you breathe out, imagine any heavy emotions or negative thoughts leaving your body from the soles of your feet.

Before interacting with them, remind yourself what you want to remember,

"I'm safe. I'm loved."

Visualise how you want the interaction to go, before it happens.

So when you go in, you're good.

Know that the trigger isn't about the person in front of you.

It's about an unmet need you have.

Don't expect this need to be met by them.

Instead, meet it yourself.

If things get out of control, that's ok too.

Have all the compassion for yourself.

You're doing your best.

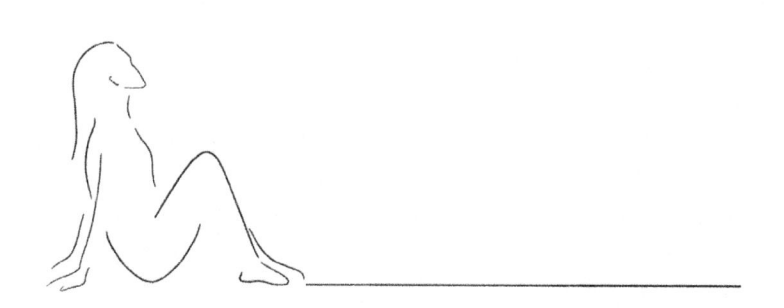

You're amazing in every way :)

Part 36 - Connect With Your Inner Child

Your inner child is a younger version of you that lives in you.

Whenever you get triggered by your parents, you can connect with your inner child and give them what they need.

Here's what you can do after having an argument with your parents:

When you're on your own, close your eyes.

Take deep breaths.

Allow your emotions to be there.

Take a moment to connect with your inner child.*

Visualise them and ask,

"How are you feeling?"

Maybe they feel hurt, angry, misunderstood or something else.

Acknowledge how they feel.

Tell them,

"I can see that you're feeling sad. It's ok to feel sad."

Then ask,

"What do you need?"

Maybe they want a hug.

Maybe they want to be comforted, knowing they're not alone and you're there with them,

"It's ok, I'm with you now. You're not on your own. I love you."

Soothe them.

Give them what they need.

You know what you need better than anyone.

You've spent all your time with yourself.

So you're the best parent for yourself.

You're amazing in every way :)

*Go to www.isiktlabar.com/guidedmeditations for the meditation to connect with your inner child.

Part 37 - Write a Letter to Your Parents

Sometimes our parents aren't able to hear us or listen to us.

In this case, write them a letter sharing how you feel.

This letter is about you, not them.

Don't blame them for what they did or didn't do.

Share how you feel.

Be vulnerable.

Be open.

Share your heart.

After sharing, also ask what you would love from them.

Make a request.

"I'd love you to hug me more."

"I'd love you to spend more time with me."

Then ask if they can do that,

"Are you open to this?"

"Is this something you'd be able to do?"

Because they might not be able to.

If they do it, great.

If they can't, that's ok too.

Our parents can only meet us at the level they have met themselves.

Sometimes they aren't able to meet your emotional needs.

Often when we communicate our needs to them, they are open to meeting them.

Doing this can feel extra vulnerable.

Know that when you're vulnerable and open in life, life gives back to you.

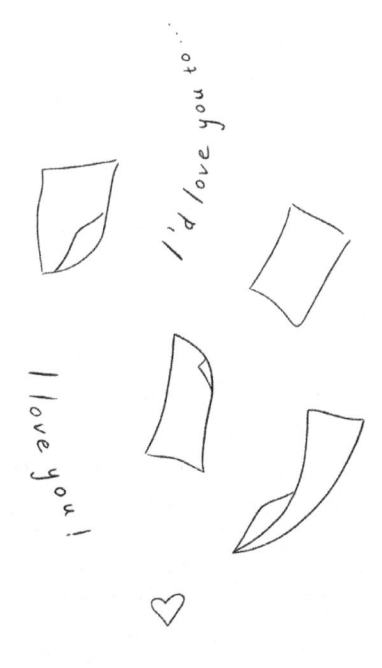

You're amazing in every way :)

I'd love you to...

I love you!

♡

Part 38 - Sharing Your Dreams With Your Parents

We look at our parents and sometimes we think they know best.

We think they have all the answers.

They're like Gods and Goddesses in our eyes.

The truth is, they're only human.

Part of growing up is realising they're not perfect.

They don't have all the answers.

They can make mistakes.

They're teaching you what they think is the right way.

They might want you to follow the career that they think is right for you.

Let's say, your mum wants you to become a doctor, but you want to be an actress.

Or you want to ask your parents to go to a boarding school, but you're worried that they won't allow you to.

Or you want to become a dancer, singer, actor, but you're feeling scared that your dad won't approve.

Before asking your parents for what you want, first visualise that your dream has come true.

Imagine you're there already.

You've done it!

You're at the boarding school.

You're a dancer.

You're singing.

Whatever your dream is.

You've already created it.

Your brain doesn't know the difference between what's real or imagined.

Use your imagination to dream, instead of using it to worry.

Then as you ask your parents, really share from your heart that you would love to do it. Share your passion for it.

Here are three steps:

Firstly, you acknowledge that you're hearing your mum's concern.

You can say:

"Mum, I understand that you want me to go to medical school. I know you want the best for me."

And she does!

But in her own way. Not in your way.

Secondly, you connect to your heart and share how much you want to become an actress, to go to boarding school or whatever it might be.

Share your passion:

"Mum, I'd love to do this. This is what I really care about. This really excites me and I believe this is the right path for me. I just know it."

Share it from genuine love, not in a begging way.

This can feel vulnerable and that's ok.

Thirdly, tell her:

"I love you so much mum. I'd love for us to find a way to talk about this with love and understanding. How does that sound?"

If you're holding back from a dream because your dad or mum might not approve, you might distance yourself from your parents and resent them for some time.

Go for your dream.

And have a great relationship with your parents.

You're amazing in every way :)

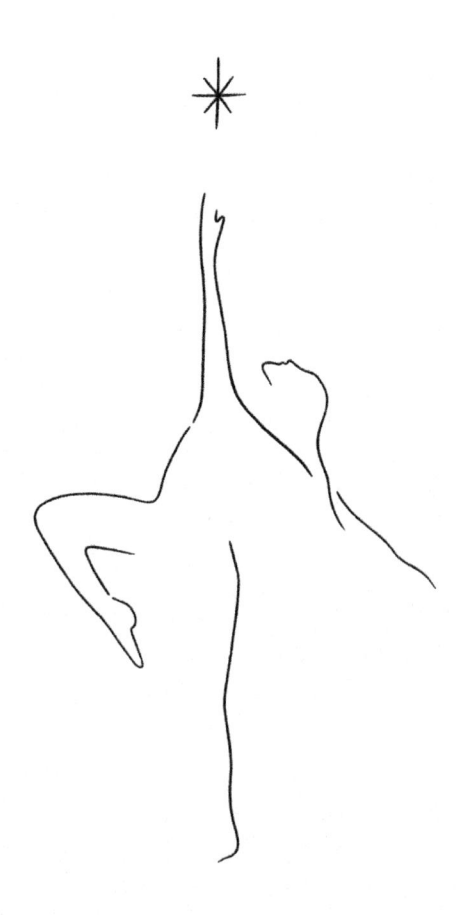

Part 39 - Parental Wounds

It's important to understand how our wounds are created to understand ourselves better.

Carl Jung, pioneering psychotherapist, explains this as the "Individuation Cycle".

When we decide to come to this world, our Soul enters our body..

In this body, we create an Ego to have an individual identity.

The Ego seeks validation.

We look to the mother (or the feminine figure) to be loved as we are.

During our earlier phase in life as babies, there is no sense of separation with the mother.

It's pure love and connection.

We want the mother to make us feel,

"I love you unconditionally, no matter what."

Then as we grow up, we look to the father (the masculine figure) to be acknowledged for what we do.

He shows us the world, challenges us and helps us find our place in the world.

We want the father to make us feel,

"Go out and do good in the world. If you need help, I'm right behind you."

Unfortunately, most of us don't get this from our parents in the way we wish we had.

This creates an unmet need.

Our Ego asks, "Why do I hurt?"

Then our Ego creates a meaning about why it hurts.

We make up what it means about us. This then turns into a belief:

"I hurt because I'm not safe. I'm not good enough, I'm not loveable. Here's the explanation."

Then the Ego makes up a strategy to compensate for the belief.

It tries to fix the belief:

"I'm not good enough." —--> If I try harder, I'll get there.

"I don't belong." —--> I'll please people to fit in, so they don't abandon me.

"It's not safe." —---> I have to be careful and need to test people first.

"I'm not loveable." —--> I have to manipulate people to get love.

This applies to our parents too.

Know that your parents are trying to do their best with what they know.

They wouldn't knowingly try to hurt or upset you.

See them through the eyes of love.

They have their own wounds as well.

You have a choice between continuing the cycle of acting from wounds.

Or breaking out of the cycle and choosing love and compassion.

It's up to you to make a new choice.

You're amazing in every way :)

ego makes up a strategy

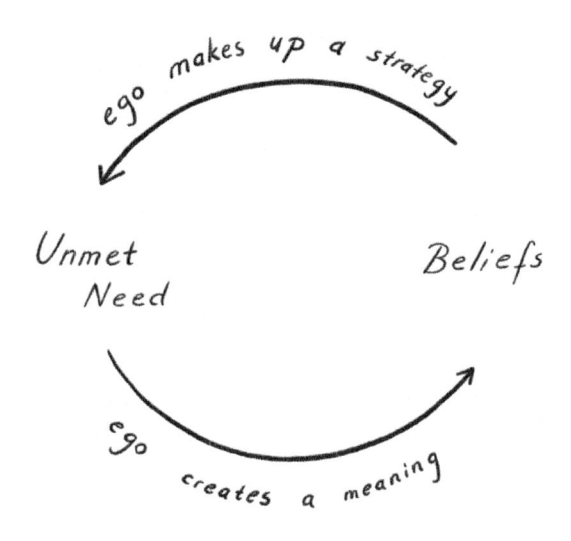

Unmet Need   Beliefs

ego creates a meaning

CONTINUE
the cycle

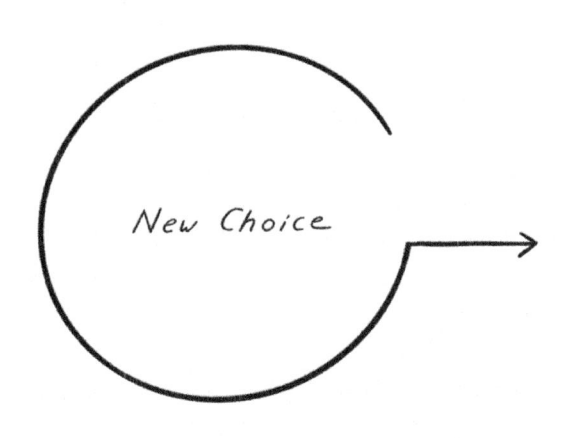

New Choice

BREAK
the cycle

Part 40 - Forgive Your Parents

It's very natural to have a wobbly relationship with your parents.

They're doing their best with the awareness they have.
jkjjjjhkjjhfjhjgk
They don't know everything.

They don't have the answer to everything.

They're just humans who didn't get their needs met either when they were little.

Knowing this, might help you feel empathy and compassion towards them.

When you start to see them as human, you start to forgive them.

When you heal and parent your inner child, you also forgive your parents.

Staying angry at someone is like holding a hot coal.

It only hurts you.

It's like holding onto a heavy, spiteful and resentful energy.

And I understand wanting to hold onto that, but it only hurts you.

When you forgive, you let go of that pain and suffering.

And you come back to the true love that was always there.

Forgiveness sets you free.

Give yourself permission to be free.

You're amazing in every way :)

Q&A 1

"Can you do one on not having a great relationship with your dad like other girls. It hurts. He has hurt me so much. But I love him as my dad."

Relationships with our parents are tricky.

It might hurt when we see other kids having a great relationship with their parents when we don't have that.

But you don't know the whole story.

From the outside, it might look great.

But when you actually take a closer look, it might look different.

Don't compare your relationship with your parents to your friends' relationship with their parents.

There's no comparison.

That's their journey.

This is your journey.

I struggled to have a good relationship with my parents as well.

It's ok to feel hurt, angry towards your parents and still love them.

Acknowledge both parts.

And if you can, allow that love to turn into forgiveness.

Can you forgive your mum and dad?

They're doing their best at any given moment.

They're only human. They're not God.

So acknowledge how you feel, let the hurt go and forgive your parents.

You're amazing in every way :)

Q&A 2

"I wanna come out to my parents but I really don't know how to, I know they're homophobic but I really wanna tell them to make myself feel better."

First of all, if this is how you feel, sharing this with your parents can be liberating.

Here's how you can do that:

(You can also use this structure with any difficult conversation you want to have with your parents.)

You can talk to them in person. Or if it's easier, you can write a letter.

You can say something along the lines of:

"Hey mum, hey dad, I want to share something with you. It's important. Is this a good time?"

When you arrange the time, sit down and say:

"I feel very nervous and scared to share this with you. I'm scared that you're going to love me less. I'm scared that you're going to disown me."

Share whatever your fears are.

Then share with them what you've been wanting to say:

"I'm gay/bi (whatever your orientation is)."

If they accept and celebrate it, great.

If they don't, that's ok.

Whatever happens, don't ever be ashamed of who you are.

To the part of you that might need to hear it, however you identify yourself as, whoever you are:

I love you so much.

You're so loved in this world.

You're so seen.

And you have a place here.

You belong.

You're amazing in every way :)

DISCLAIMER:

Only come out to your parents if it's safe to do so in your country and family. Find out if it's safe to come out in your country here:

https://www.humandignitytrust.org/lgbt-the-law/map-of-criminalisation

Abuse is never acceptable. If you're in a situation where you need help, you can seek support through this website:

https://childhelplineinternational.org/helplines/

Q&A 3

"The thing is my parents are against that I wanna be an actress :("

Your parents are only doing what they think is good for you. They're coming from a different generation with different backgrounds.

It can be helpful to listen to what they have to say.

Take in what they're saying, but always ask yourself:

"What would I love to do?"

Modelling, acting, writing songs, writing books, dancing, whatever it might be, follow that!

Never give up on that.

You'll be successful at it because you love it and do it with such passion, they'll be so proud. They'll only see it when you do it.

Once you're 18, you're an adult. You're free to live the life you'd love to live.

So hold onto that dream of becoming an actress, singer, model, dancer, whatever it might be.

And follow that.

You're amazing in every way :)

RELATIONSHIPS

Part 41 - Choose The Love You Want

Getting clear on your relationship vision is super important.

This is imagining what kind of connection you would like to share with someone.

Close your eyes and take three deep breaths.

Connect with your heart.

Ask yourself,

"What would I love to experience in an intimate relationship?"

Maybe it's sharing love.

Maybe it's having fun together.

Having deep conversations.

Going on adventures or something else.

How does that make you feel?

Ask yourself, "What's the emotion of that?"

Maybe it's joy, love, peace, freedom or something else.

Don't focus on how the other person looks.

Focus on how you feel with them.

You might be looking for someone who has blonde hair and miss a beautiful connection with a dark haired person sitting right next to you.

So, when you're getting to know someone, remember your vision.

Notice how you feel when you're with them.

Don't lose yourself in the other person.

Stay connected to yourself and what you want.

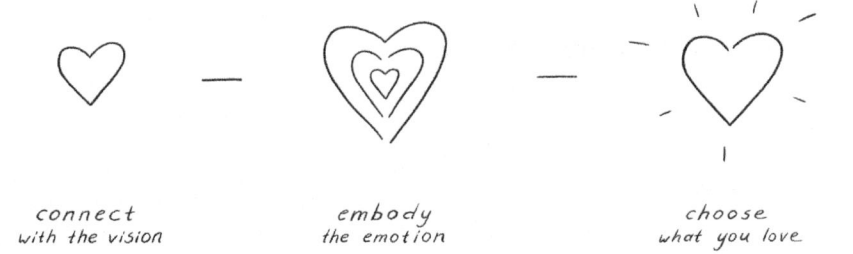

You're amazing in every way :)

connect with the vision — *embody the emotion* — *choose what you love*

Part 42 - Don't Repeat the Past

People often enter into relationships trying to get their unmet needs from childhood met.

That is not what relationships are for.

We're meant to meet that need ourselves.

Then, going into relationships becomes a choice, not a need.

You might be experiencing similar patterns with different people.

You don't have to repeat the past and the same heartbreaks.

Feel the pain, make a new choice towards what you would love in a relationship.

And take action from that place to create a new reality.

You're amazing in every way :)

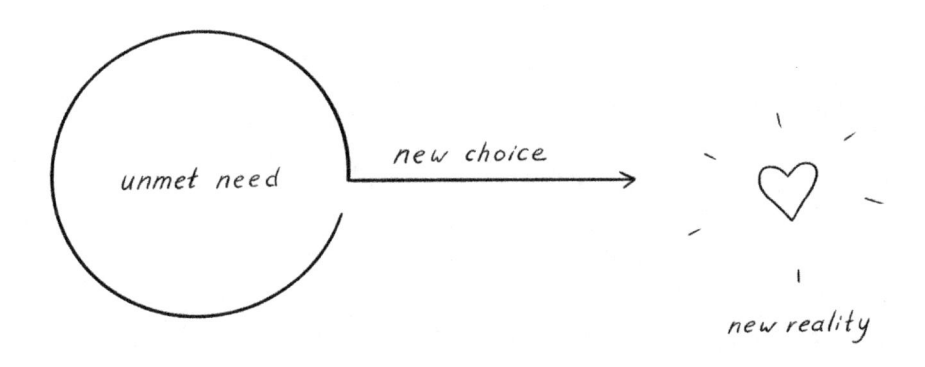

unmet need → new choice → ♡
                          new reality

Part 43 - Is Your Crush Real?

When you have a crush on someone, check whether it's a projection or your true feelings.

A projection is creating an image of someone based on who you think they are, instead of seeing them as they are.

When you have an idealised version of someone like your crush, this bypasses who they actually are.

When they show you who they are, you might feel disappointment.

I had a crush on a boy when I was about 12.

He was a popular guy in our school.

I wasn't popular, so I idealised him.

One evening our parents hung out.

This guy and I watched something together.

I got to see the real him.

I found that he wasn't who I thought he was.

Then I felt disappointed.

My crush ended shortly after that and I was free.

That was the first time I saw how people might not be who I idealise them to be.

It was a valuable lesson.

So check whether you're in distortion or in reality.

You're amazing in every way :)

Part 44 - Share Your Feelings With Your Crush

Sharing your feelings to your crush can be terrifying.

But if you're certain about how you feel about them, why would you hold back?

There are three steps in how you can share your feelings with them:

1. Share how you feel

2. Make an offer

3. Wait for the answer

If you aren't close to them,

"Hey, I know that we don't know each other that well. I've been seeing you around and I think you're amazing (or beautiful, whatever you want to say). I'd love to get to know you more. Are you free after school?"

If you're already friends or you know them a bit,

'Hey, do you have a moment? I'd like to share something with you. (When they say yes) I feel nervous to share this, but recently I've been having feelings for you. I'd love to explore this connection. Would you be open to that?"

You got this!

You're amazing in every way :)

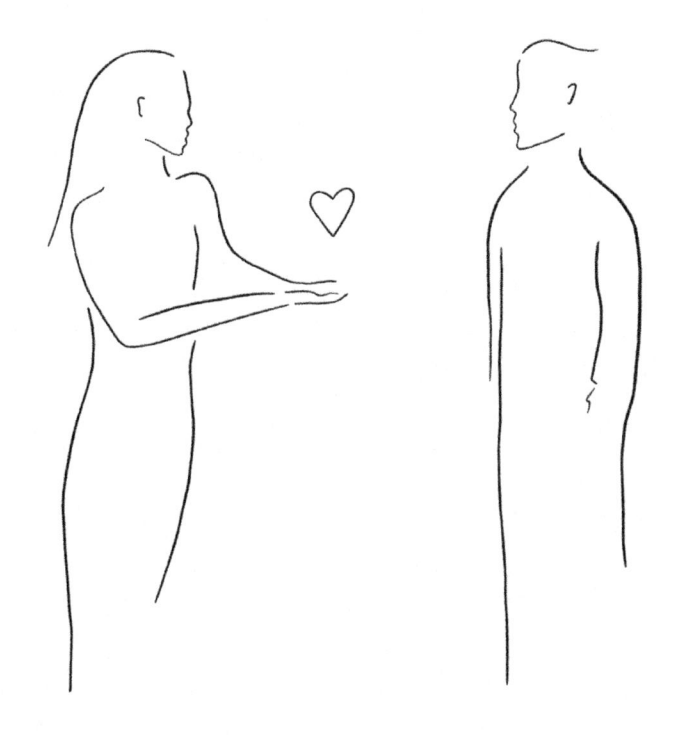

Part 45 - Be Brave In Love

Be brave in love.

When you lean into love, life opens up for you.

Take risks.

Be vulnerable.

Share your heart.

If that person doesn't meet you there, that's ok.

You've kept your heart open.

And life will meet you there.

It's inevitable.

You're amazing in every way :)

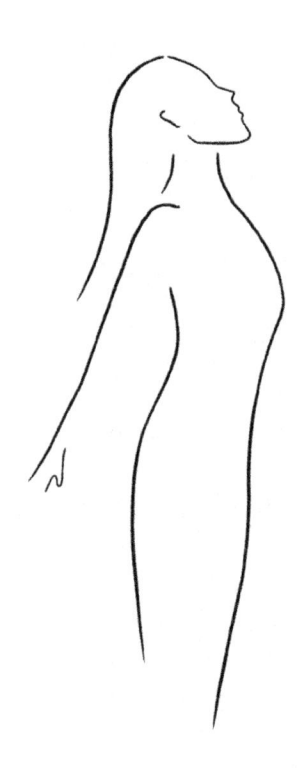

Part 46 - Don't Overstretch Your Heart

When you're getting to know someone, stay connected to your heart.

Keep asking yourself,

"What does my heart want?"

"What do I need in a relationship?"

Honour your needs, before going for what you want.

Maybe you need to feel safe to trust someone.

Maybe you need honesty and openness.

Then what you might want is fun and adventure.

Or having deep conversations sharing similar interests.

If you don't like someone's vibe, you don't have to connect with them. You also don't have to open up straight away.

You can take as much time as you need, until you feel ready to share your heart.

Don't cross your own boundary and overstretch your heart to meet someone else's.

Honour your heart. Be with those who will hold your heart.

You're amazing in every way :)

Part 47 - Don't Look To Be Saved

You're not a victim to be saved.

Growing up as girls, we're fed this fairy tale story of a prince charming coming and saving us.

So we might idealise a guy saving us from our pain.

This might keep you in waiting mode.

Being saved isn't going to come from someone else.

It's going to come from you.

You are your own hero.

Create your own story.

You're amazing in every way :)

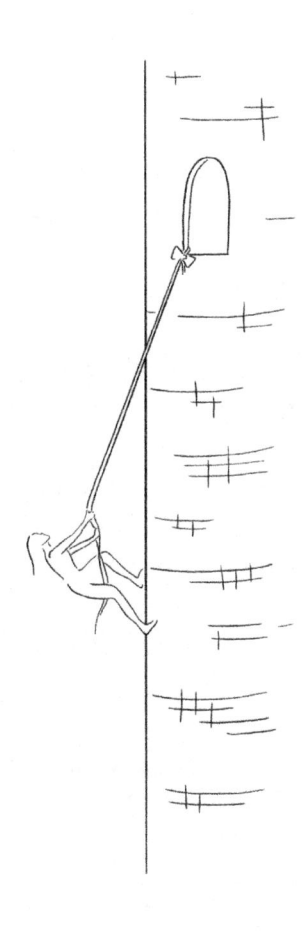

Part 48 - Being Chosen by a Boy

Your main goal in life isn't to be chosen by a boy.

This takes your power away.

You can choose what your main goal in your life is.

It can be truly living, enjoying your life or sharing your gifts with the world.

Writing, dancing, singing, teaching, acting, etc.

Whatever fills you up and whatever brings you alive, go and do that.

Don't worry about being chosen or not.

Choose yourself.

The right person will come along when you're busy enjoying your life.

You're amazing in every way :)

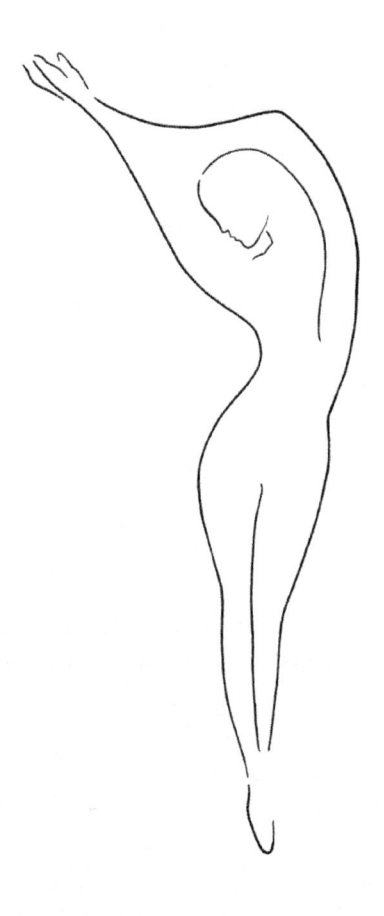

Part 49 - Rejection

I know it hurts when you're being rejected.

However it actually doesn't mean anything about you.

It just shows that what you want and what the other person wants are different.

It doesn't mean you're not lovable.

It doesn't mean you're not good enough.

Rejection is two truths not being aligned.

There's nothing wrong with you.

You are loved.

You are enough.

If you keep putting your heart out there courageously, keeping yourself open, sooner or later you'll receive everything you want.

You're amazing in every way :)

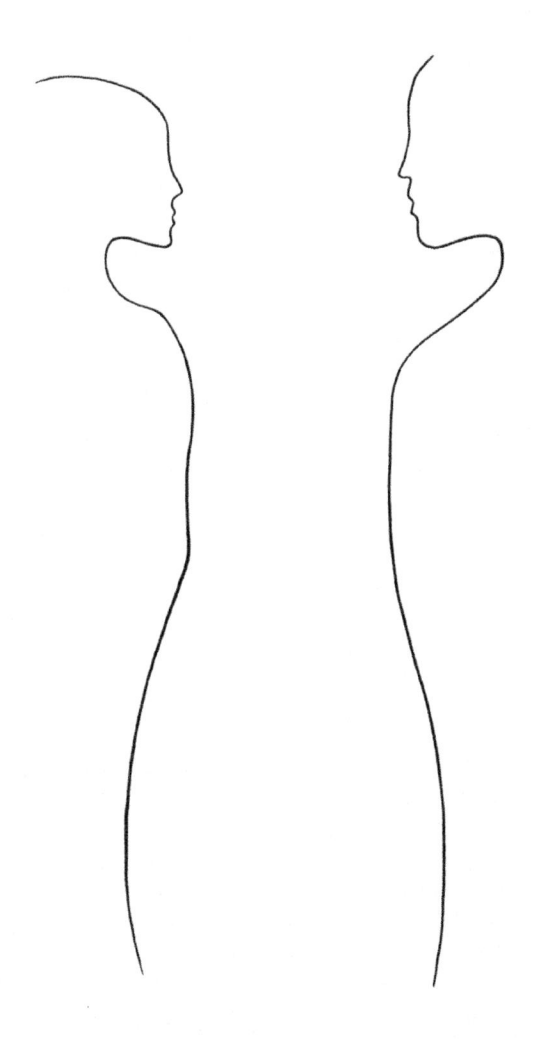

Part 50 - Your Worth is Not About Your Looks

Your worth is not defined by how pretty you are.

How you look is only one aspect of you.

There's so much more to you.

There's your intelligence.

Your intuition.

Your heart.

Your creativity.

Your humour.

Your talents.

Your ideas.

Your dreams.

Your passions.

And more.

Focus on all of them rather than just focusing on how you look.

You're amazing in every way :)

Part 51 - Speak Your Truth

Speak your truth.

Express how you feel.

You can say "no" to people.

You're not at the mercy of others.

If you've been connecting with someone and you want to end that connection but you also don't want to be rude, here's what you can say in your own words:

"Hey lovely, it has been beautiful spending some time together and getting to know you. I'm clear in what I'm looking for and I'm not feeling that in our connection. Thank you for the time we shared together. Wishing you the best."

Don't ghost them.

Don't avoid them.

Speak your truth.

Honesty and transparency sets both of you free.

This way, they know where they stand.

You know where you stand.

It creates clarity.

It's also respectful and honouring to the human being in front of you.

Be honest.

You're amazing in every way :)

Part 52 - Getting Over Someone

Breakups are painful.

Maybe you were in a long term relationship and you broke up.

Maybe you were connecting with a boy for a while and the connection ended.

There are three parts to getting over them:

1. Feel how you're feeling

Really give yourself full permission to feel that sadness, grief, anger, frustration, jealousy or whatever's there.

To do this part you can put on some sad music*.

Give yourself 30 to 60 minutes to cry it out and feel.

Let it out.

Putting a time limit will contain the energy.

You can also let them go by writing them a letter.

Don't send the letter to them.

Write it out for yourself.

Say everything you want to say to them.

Or you can do this in a voice note you record for yourself.

Keep talking and sharing how you feel.

Breathe through it.

You can do this as many times as you like.

And then let them go.

You can also move it out, dance it out.

2. Make a completion on the connection

Moving on from a connection without completion is like leaving open tabs on your computer.

It might drain your energy making you feel tired.

Ask yourself,

"What happened in the connection?

"What did we share?"

This allows you to reflect on the highs and lows of the connection.

Then ask,

"What have I learnt?"

Maybe you learnt what you want and don't want.

Even if there was a heartbreak, you gained learnings from it.

Then ask, "What am I letting go of now?"

Maybe there was self-doubt, insecurities or something they said that hurt you.

You can move on by letting go of the things that aren't serving you with a grateful heart.

3. Focus on what you love

As you let go, choose where you want to direct your energy now.

Focus on you.

Ask yourself,

"What do I love doing?"

"What brings me alive?"

"What's my passion?"

Maybe it's writing, reading, music, dancing etc.

Shift your focus from the victim, "poor me" place to the creator, "following my joy" place.

This brings your attention back to yourself.

It's important to do these three parts.

Feel your feelings as they come up.

And keep focusing on yourself, what you love.

Give yourself lots of time and compassion.

When your heart is open, it heals faster.

When it's closed, it's harder for the emotions to move through.

Keep your heart open and love even more next time.

I've had many heartbreaks.

Every time, I loved deeper.

That's what the heart does.

It just wants to love.

You will love again.

You will be loved again.

You're amazing in every way :)

PAST	PRESENT	FUTURE
♡	✳	🕊
allow yourself to feel	what did we share? what have I learnt? what am I letting go?	what do I love?

* You can scan and check out my "Grief" playlist on Spotify. Set 30 minutes aside and put on the playlist. Feel and move through your emotions. Make sure you breathe, shake your body off and make sounds.

Part 53 - Conscious Uncoupling

We start relationships with love.

It is also possible to end them with love.

You can end them with even more love than when you started.

There is a term created by Katherine Woodward Thomas, "conscious uncoupling".

It involves letting each other go with love.

Instead of becoming strangers overnight or hating each other, you are supporting one another as you complete your relationship with love.

If you're ending a relationship, you can do the things you used to love doing together one final time.

This could be going to the movies together.

Going to your favourite place together.

Having deep and meaningful conversations etc.

It might have a bittersweet feel to it, that's ok.

Allow the emotions that come up.

Share with each other what you taught one another.

Share what you're grateful for from the time you had together.

Not all relationships are meant to last forever.

Just because a relationship ended, it doesn't mean it failed.

Quite the contrary, maybe through the time you shared together, your heart has grown bigger.

Maybe you got to know yourself better.

Allow your relationship to be whatever it wants to be.

And when the time comes to let each other go, let each other go.

At that point, you can decide to have some space, like a month or more, so that your body and heart can register the breakup in that alone time.

Make sure you're on the same page that the relationship is complete.

So that neither of you are wanting to get back together.

After the space apart, check in to see if you're ready to be friends after this relationship.

If you don't want that, that's ok too.

Love between you two doesn't have to die.

It can deepen.

Love never goes away.

It transforms.

Let it transform.

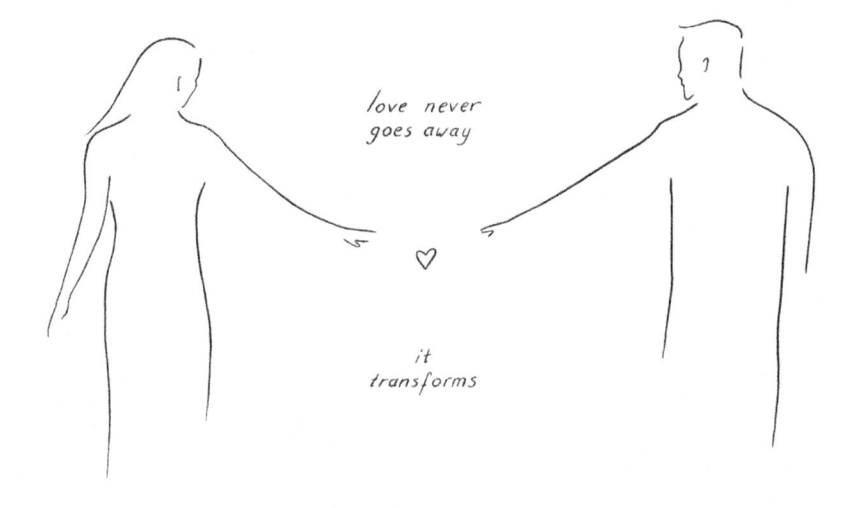

You're amazing in every way :)

love never goes away

it transforms

Q&A 1

"What if someone you thought was your friend took advantage of you and your body. He didn't step back when I told him to stop kissing and touching me."

If someone is touching your body or kissing you and not stopping when you tell them to stop, this isn't ok.

Having said that, I'd like to share where this behaviour might be coming from.

So that we can understand it instead of shaming it.

The first reason is porn.

Porn doesn't really teach you about how to communicate your desires, consent, boundaries and your needs.

It's not the best sex education.

It's not real. It's acting.

Physical intimacy is also about building trust, talking about emotions, fears and vulnerabilities.

It's not just physical. It's about two souls meeting.

Boys who grow up watching porn get conditioned to think, "Oh this is how men and women interact."

Girls too, girls watching porn have the same conditioning, or any other gender.

The second reason is the masculine and feminine balance.

Regardless of our gender, we have two energy channels within us, one that moves in an outward direction, 'yang energy' and one that moves in an inward direction, 'yin energy'.

In our society, boys are encouraged to be more outward, yang - to do, achieve, get what you want, be a man. It's linear and more focused.

Whereas girls are encouraged to be more inward, yin - to be nice, likeable, and more loving, to not rock the boat and to be good girls.

This creates men who are not in touch with their emotions and women who don't know what they want.

We need both the feminine and the masculine, yin and yang.

In a situation where someone is physically touching you without your consent, they might be believing that's what a man does, they get what they want.

As a girl, you might be believing and thinking to yourself in that moment - girls do as they're told.

In this scenario, as Kasia Urbaniak, writer of *Unbound: A Woman's Guide to Power*, shares in her work, what you need to do is go from inward energy to the outward.

The best way you can do this is to direct the attention onto them.

If they're kissing and touching you, the attention is on you.

You need to direct it back by asking a bold question.

Something like:

"What do you think you're doing?"

"Who do you think you are?"

That will baffle them. They will go, "What?!"

In that short space you have, you push them, leave, scream and you remove yourself from that situation.

If this person is a friend, later on you can open up a conversation and say:

"Hey, I'd like to share how I felt about what happened. Would you be open to hearing it?"

Because that will not only allow you to express how you feel, it will also give them awareness and that's powerful.

I want you to know that you're powerful and you deserve to be treated how you want to be treated.

You're not at the mercy of others.

You're amazing in every way :)

inwards ⟶ outwards

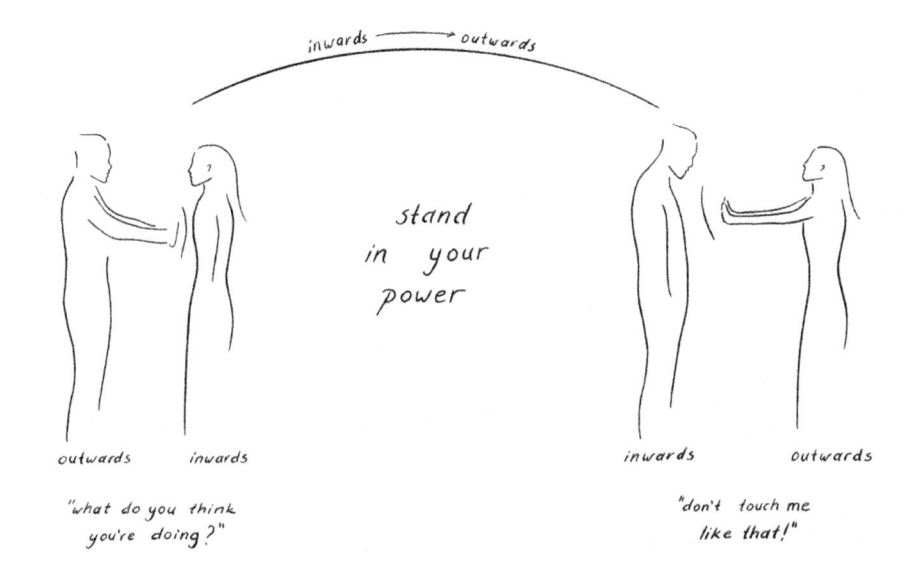

stand
in your
power

outwards   inwards

"what do you think
you're doing?"

inwards   outwards

"don't touch me
like that!"

Q&A 2

"I just realised my main goal was to be chosen by this boy. I tried becoming a better person for him but not myself. Thank you."

When we put someone else in the centre of our world, they take our power away.

You are the centre of your own world.

You are the leader of your own life.

This is your life!

Become a better version of yourself for you, not for anyone else.

Everything else you want and everything else you love will follow.

You're amazing in every way :)

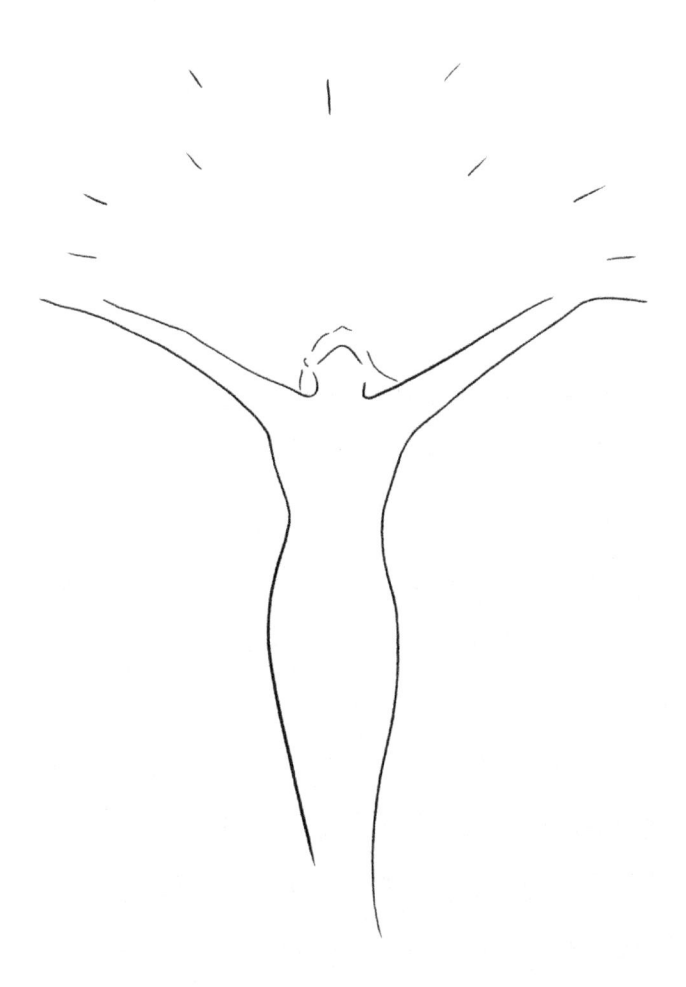

Q&A 3

"All my life I've been in love with this boy that keeps ignoring me. I've tried for so long (years) to let him go. What do you think about this?"

Often when we're in love with someone we barely know, we're not in love with them.

We're in love with the idea of them.

The idea of what this potential relationship could be.

Maybe it's the idea that they're going to make everything better.

Maybe it's the idea that you'll be loved by them.

We're often in love with the idea, and not the person.

If we really see them as they are, it sets us free.

Maybe get to know the person, find out who they really are.

If you still feel the same, you can even share your feelings with them and see what happens.

You're amazing in every way :)

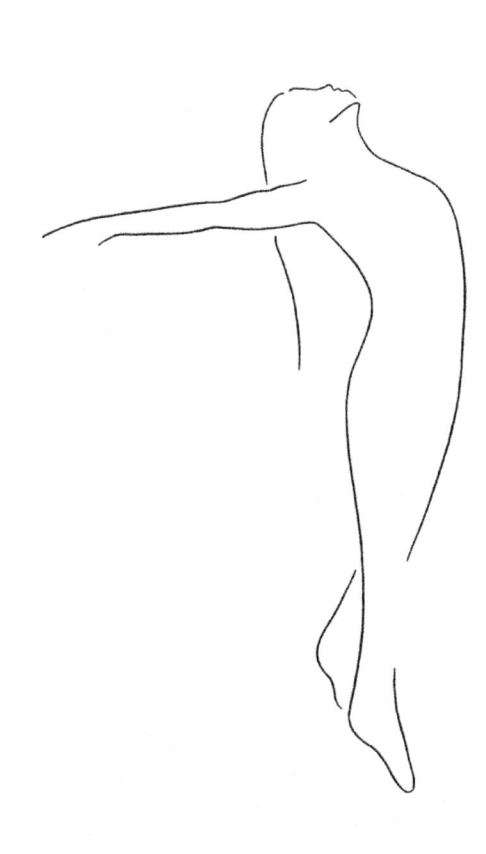

EMOTIONS

Part 54 - What Are Emotions?

Emotions are energy in motion.

We all feel them.

Your mind might judge them as good or bad emotions.

They just are.

Feeling emotions is part of being human.

There's absolutely nothing wrong with you.

I'd like to see emotions as lighter and darker ones.

Lighter ones are emotions like joy, love and gratitude.

Darker ones are like fear, shame, guilt, sadness etc.

They're just denser or lighter.

Don't judge how you're feeling and allow them.

You're amazing in every way :)

light   dense

dense   light

EMOTIONS

joy   love   gratitude

shame   guilt   sadness

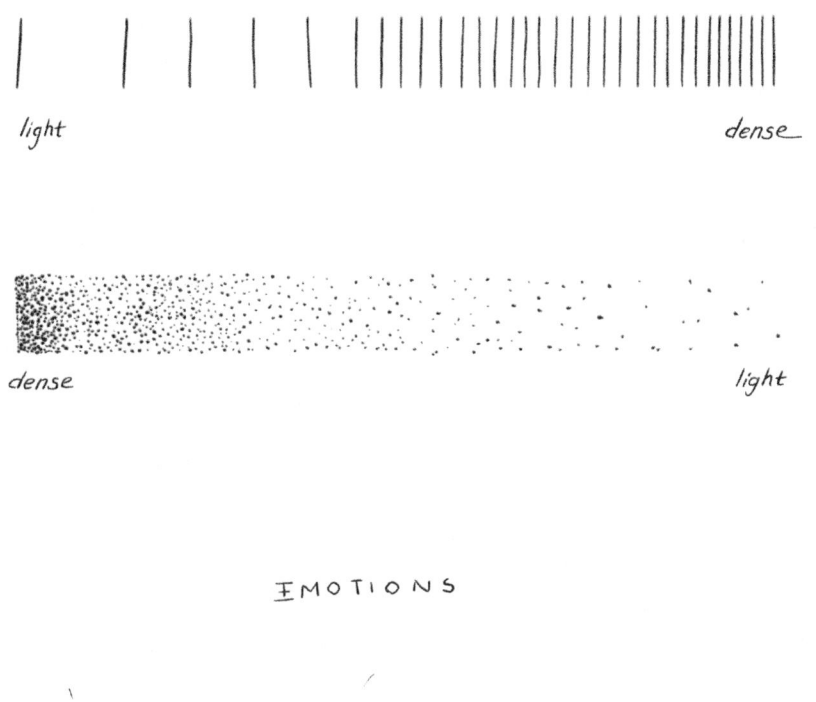

Part 55 - Process Your Emotions

Moving through your emotions is like moving through waves in the sea.

The deeper you go into your sadness, the higher your joy will be too.

In 2018, my dad died suddenly from a heart attack.

Feeling and going through the grief opened my heart more and made my joy even deeper.

My laughter changed.

Whatever you're feeling, really sit with it.

Whether you're feeling sad, anxious or scared.

The only way out is through.

Don't avoid feeling by distracting yourself.

Instead, close your eyes, take a deep breath in and just notice however you're feeling.

Breathe through it.

Often the mind thinking about the feeling makes it worse.

When you actually sit with it, it might be painful for a bit.

Then it's actually ok.

Know that you're not alone in feeling that.

You didn't come here just to experience joy, gratitude, bliss etc.

You've come here to experience the full spectrum of being human, feeling all the emotions.

You're human and you're meant to feel.

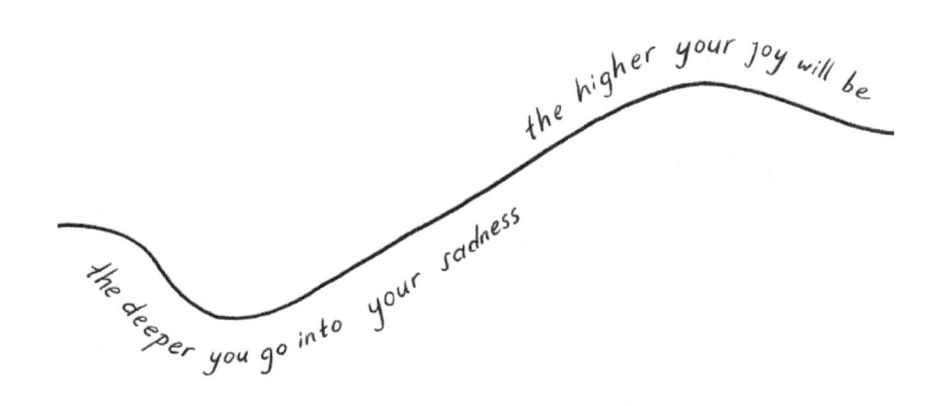

You're amazing in every way :)

the deeper you go into your sadness the higher your joy will be

Part 56 - You're Allowed To Feel

You're allowed to feel all the emotions.

Sad, angry, frustrated, guilty, ashamed.

Maybe you easily allow yourself to feel joy.

But sadness or anger might be emotions you struggle to feel and express.

We're not really taught how to feel the uncomfortable emotions in a healthy way.

When you allow yourself to feel, you move through the emotions faster.

Welcome them like waves moving through you.

Accept them.

Don't judge them.

When you judge, you block them from flowing easily.

Allow yourself to feel.

You're amazing in every way :)

Part 57 - Let Go Of Emotions

Sometimes it takes us a while to process emotions.

Sometimes it can take a moment.

In fact, we have the ability to move through emotions super fast.

Just like dropping a pen, you can let them go.

It takes a decision.

There is a modality called the Sedona Method created by Hale Dwoskin.

You start by bringing your awareness to the issue that you would like to feel better about.

Allow yourself to feel whatever you are feeling at this moment.

Then choose to let go of the emotion.

Ask yourself and answer these questions,

1. "Could I allow and welcome this feeling?"

2. "Would I let the feeling go?"

3. "When would I let it go?"

If the answer is "no," or if you are not sure, ask yourself,

"Would I rather have this feeling, or would I rather be free?"

Even if the answer is still "no," move onto the next question.

Let go when you're ready.

Make sure to breathe as you answer them, "yes", "no" or whatever feels true.

Then welcome in whatever emotion you'd like to welcome in like joy, ease and connection.

Repeat as many times as needed.

You're amazing in every way :)

Could I allow and welcome this feeling?

Would I let the feeling go?

When would I let it go?

Part 58 - Fear

When you have a dream, it's very natural to feel scared.

The more we resist something, the more important and true it is to follow it.

This is one of my favourite quotes by Joseph Campbell:

"The cave you fear to enter holds the treasure you seek."

Go in the direction of your fear, not away from it.

Don't let the fear stop you.

Lean into it.

Absolutely go for it.

You're amazing in every way :)

Part 59 - Jealousy

Jealousy is a very natural emotion.

Here are three steps to move through jealousy:

The first step is owning and acknowledging that you're jealous.

There's nothing shameful about feeling jealous.

Let go of any embarrassment about it.

We all feel it.

The second step is asking yourself,

"What am I jealous of?"

Really sit with it and find what it is.

Maybe you're jealous of how loving someone is.

Maybe you're jealous of how outgoing and social someone is.

Maybe you're jealous of how free someone is.

We're often jealous of what we also want to have and embody.

Once you find what you're jealous of, the third step is to cultivate that in you.

Whatever the quality they have and you're jealous of, ask yourself,

"How can I be more of that?"

"How can I create more of that in my life?"

This is how you transform jealousy.

Let it teach you.

Let yourself grow from it.

Own the jealousy, find what you're jealous of and then cultivate it.

You're amazing in every way :)

Part 60 - Negative Thoughts

It's ok to have negative thoughts.

It's not about trying to get rid of them.

It's about having a healthy relationship with them.

It's about learning to be with them in a non-judgemental way.

Know that they're just thoughts.

They don't define who you are.

They're not even real.

Sometimes having the fear and anxiety around having the negative thoughts can actually be worse than having the thoughts themselves.

So know that it's ok to have them.

Everyone has negative thoughts.

And when they arrive, just notice:

"Oh, here's a negative thought."

After acknowledging these thoughts, imagine yourself rising above them.

See them from a higher perspective.

From that point, ask yourself:

"What's the truth from here?"

"What would a positive thought say about this?"

That will help you to see that negative thoughts are actually not true.

They're just as made up as other thoughts.

So you can make up a new, healthier thought.

See them as clouds going in and out just like the feelings.

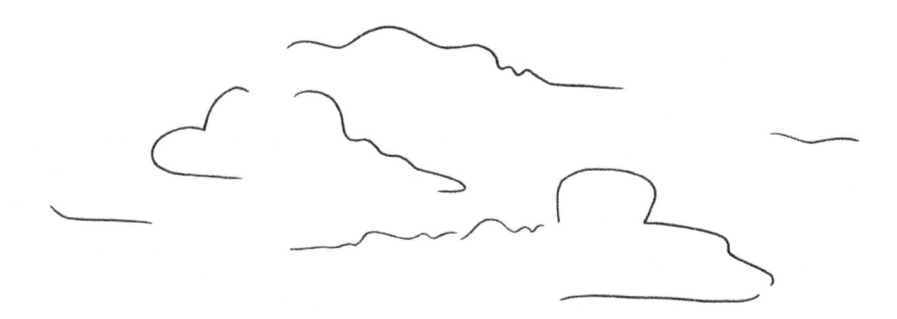

You're amazing in every way :)

Part 61 - Share Feelings

Sharing how you feel is a strength.

It's not a weakness.

When you share your feelings vulnerably, you're actually being brave.

You can share your feelings by saying:

"I feel very nervous sharing this right now,.."

And then share.

If the person you're sharing your feelings with doesn't honour your feelings, that's ok.

You are honouring your feelings by sharing them openly.

That's what matters.

Your feelings are valid.

If you feel you're bothering people when you share how you feel, you can ask for their permission:

"I'd love to share with you how I'm feeling. Is that ok?"

"Would you be open to hearing how I'm feeling?"

That gives them a space to say "yes" or "no".

If they say "yes", then you know you're not bothering them.

You asked for their permission and got it.

If they say "no", that's ok too.

It's their job to decide if they want to listen or not.

You're amazing in every way :)

Part 62 - You're Worthy

You're worthy as you are.

You deserve all the good things life has to offer you.

You don't have to earn your worth.

It's inherently there.

You're already incredible as you are.

You deserve it all.

You're amazing in every way :)

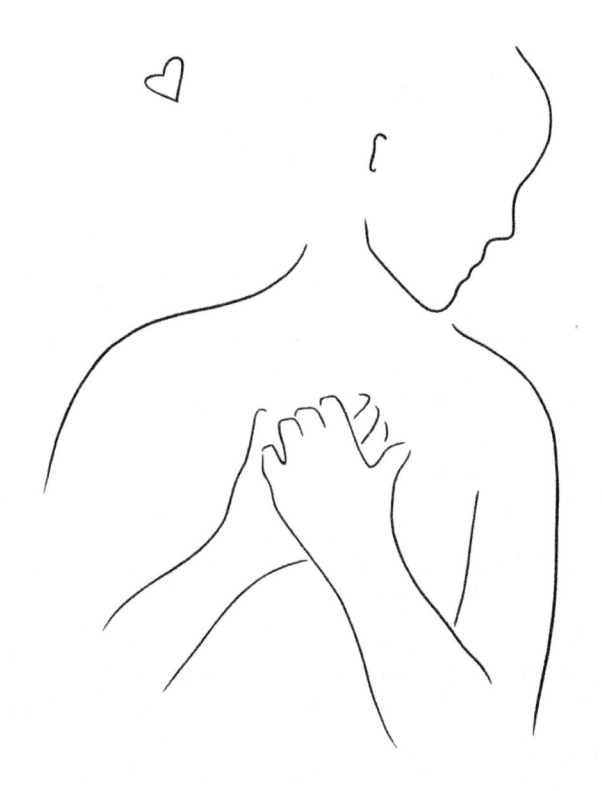

Part 63 - Feeling Lonely

Loneliness is something we all feel at some point in our lives.

When you feel lonely, you feel like you're the only person in the world feeling this way.

Know that you're not alone.

Notice the difference between feeling lonely and being on your own.

When you're feeling lonely, it's a feeling of separation and isolation.

When you're on your own, you have a whole world inside you.

There's richness there.

Notice the loneliness, see what you might need and give yourself that.

Know that you're so loved, held and supported.*

You're never on your own.

You're amazing in every way :)

*Go to www.isiktlabar.com/guidedmeditations for the meditation to feel connected with the world.

Part 64 - Be Kind To Yourself

It's ok to feel bad about yourself.

How you feel about yourself is often not a true reflection of who you truly are.

Often we can easily see the good in others.

But we can struggle to see it in ourselves.

Imagine if you were your best friend.

How would you talk to yourself?

What would you say to yourself?

Treat yourself like a good friend.

You're amazing in every way :)

Part 65 - Feedback

When you fail, it doesn't make you a failure.

It's just feedback on what didn't work.

It's just information.

Take the feedback, make the adjustment and keep going.

You're amazing in every way :)

Part 66 - Learn From Past Mistakes

It's ok to make mistakes.

That's how you learn.

You don't have to put pressure on yourself to get it right the first time.

You might feel a lot of pressure from your parents, school, teachers, whoever else, to do well.

Though as you make mistakes, that's how you learn.

Allow yourself to make mistakes.

Everyone makes mistakes.

No one's perfect.

Know that we're all human.

That is how we grow.

Seeing the lesson in a past mistake is a great way to let go of the mistake.

Then the mistake gives you a gift as you move on.

Even if you make a mistake, you win.

Whatever the experience was, ask yourself:

"What did this teach me?"

"What have I learnt from this?"

Don't beat yourself up.

Take the learning and let the rest go.

Don't give more energy to it than what you've already given.

When you make a mistake and you learn from it, you actually haven't failed.

You gained a valuable lesson.

Don't be scared of making mistakes.

That will give you so much freedom.

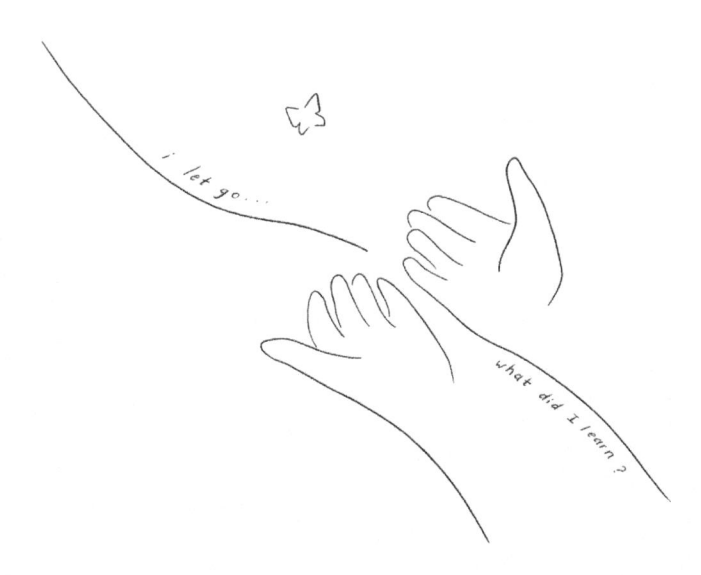

You're amazing in every way :)

Part 67 - You're Loved

I love you.

I love you.

I love you so much!

You are so loved.

Sometimes it can feel like you aren't loved but there is always love.

The sun is always behind the clouds, even when you don't see it.

Feelings will come and go.

Don't always believe them.

Don't make them mean anything.

Even at times when you don't feel loved by your parents or friends, you're always loved.

You're amazing in every way :)

Part 68 - You're Not Too Much

At some point in your life, maybe you felt sharing your feelings was bad.

Maybe you had parents or caretakers who weren't able to understand or care for your emotions.

Because they probably weren't able to understand or care for theirs either.

This may have made you decide your emotions are too much.

That's not true.

Your emotions aren't too much.

You're not too much.

The truth is you feel deeply.

That's a beautiful thing.

Own your sensitivity and depth.

You're amazing in every way :)

Part 69 - Love Yourself In Loneliness

You might be going through a hard time right now.

You might feel like no one understands you.

Your family doesn't understand you.

Your friends don't understand you.

It's ok to feel lonely.

There is no shame in feeling lonely.

Everyone feels lonely.

Often when we feel lonely, we think we're the only ones. We're not.

It's such a human thing.

When you feel lonely, give yourself a hug.

Hold yourself, feel your own touch and tell yourself,

"I love you. You're so loved."

Even if you don't feel like it, just say those words and hold yourself.

Soothe the part of you that feels lonely.

You're amazing in every way :)

Part 70 - Trust People

Your intuition will tell you who to trust.

You'll get a good feeling about someone.

Trust that feeling.

Or you'll get some bad vibes from someone.

Trust your inner knowing.

Sometimes you take the risk.

If they break your trust, don't trust them again.

Unless they are willing to earn your trust again through their changed behaviours.

After that, don't make an assumption that no one is to be trusted.

That was only true for that one specific person.

Don't turn it into a general assumption.

It doesn't mean you can never trust anyone ever again.

There are beautiful and trustworthy people in the world.

May they show you what loyalty and true friendship mean.

You're amazing in every way :)

trust

Part 71 - This Will Pass

Maybe life is a little tough right now.

Maybe it sucks right now.

But things change.

Things don't always stay the same.

Know that this will pass.

Remember the saying by Thomas Fuller,

"The night is darkest just before dawn."

Be patient.

Things will get better.

You're amazing in every way :)

Q&A 1

"I have already lost the trust in myself. It's really challenging. How can I fix it?"

If you've lost trust in yourself, that's ok.

You can rebuild it again.

You might be told constantly by your teachers, parents, friends that "you don't know", that you're "too young to know what you want."

That's not true for everyone.

If you know, you know.

That has nothing to do with your age.

When you're constantly told these messages of "you don't know", you tell yourself:

"Oh well, maybe they're right. Maybe I don't know."

Then you start losing trust in yourself.

Imagine a part of you that truly trusts itself.

Ask that part what it wants to say.

Follow that.

You're amazing in every way :)

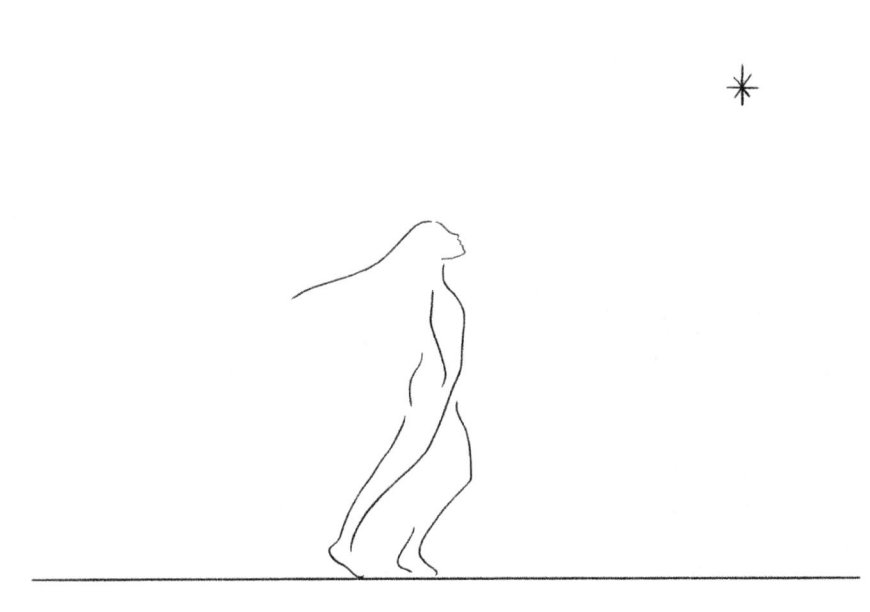

SELF-CARE

Part 72 - Self-Care Is Important

Your self-care is everything.

It's your physical, mental, emotional and spiritual health.

Physical health is how good you feel in your body: your wellbeing around eating, sleeping, working out.

Mental health is what you feed your mind.

The same way you wouldn't eat garbage, don't expose your mind to things you don't want to feed from.

For example, on social media, follow the accounts that make you feel good and are healthy for your mind.

Emotional health is how well you process emotions and not let them stagnate within you.

Spiritual health is how connected you feel to your essence and a higher power guiding and supporting you.

Self-care is the way you look after yourself holistically.

Pay attention to self-care so you feel more like yourself.

So that you feel more alive.

So you operate well.

A flower dies, when you don't water it.

A car breaks down, if you don't get it checked for a while.

Why would you be any different?

These are the life skills to have.

This is your life.

Take responsibility for it and make it the best life ever.

You're amazing in every way :)

Part 73 - Learn To Look After Yourself

If you feel low, you probably haven't moved, slept or ate well.

You might worry about what's wrong with you.

But it might simply be that you haven't slept enough or haven't eaten in a while.

Ask yourself when you feel low,

"Have I eaten today?"

"Have I drank water today?"

"Have I taken a shower today?"

"Have I gone outside today?"

"Have I moved today?"

"Did I go to bed at a decent time yesterday?"

If you said "no", do them. And see how you feel after.

You feeling low might just be a structural problem.

If you said "yes", then you know that it's something else.

You can move onto exploring that without being hard on yourself.

You're amazing in every way :)

EAT — MOVE — SLEEP — REST

Part 74 - Replace Addictions With Connections

Addictions happen because of a lack of connection.

You might be scrolling on social media or eating chocolate to feel connected and loved.

We all do some form of this in our lives.

I do this too.

This messes with the dopamine levels in your brain.

Instead of going outside for substances, go within.

Give yourself what you need.

Put on some calming music.

Create a loving space for yourself.

Daydream, read, draw, or simply be with yourself in your loving and peaceful bubble.

Or call up a friend to meet up.

You're amazing in every way :)

Part 75 - Make Your Bed

Make your bed first thing in the morning.

This gives your brain dopamine and helps you complete tasks later on in the day.

Starting tasks and not completing them can create overwhelm.

It's like a tab that you leave open on your laptop.

It slows everything down.

When you start tasks and you complete them, you feel so much better.

So make your bed when you wake up.

This is great for your own wellbeing.

And your own mental health.

You're amazing in every way :)

Part 76 - Drink Water

Have a bottle with you throughout the day.

This way you'll remember to drink water.

Sometimes when you feel down or tired, you might just be dehydrated.

If you have it next to you where you can see, you're more likely to drink it.

It will help you feel so much better and energised.

You're amazing in every way :)

Part 77 - Tidy Room

Tidy your room.

I know you might not want to tidy your room.

But it's really good for your mental health.

Do it for you.

Not for anyone else.

It will help you think clearer.

It will help you feel more peaceful.

It will help with your anxiety too.

Think of it as organising your environment to organise your mind.

You're amazing in every way :)

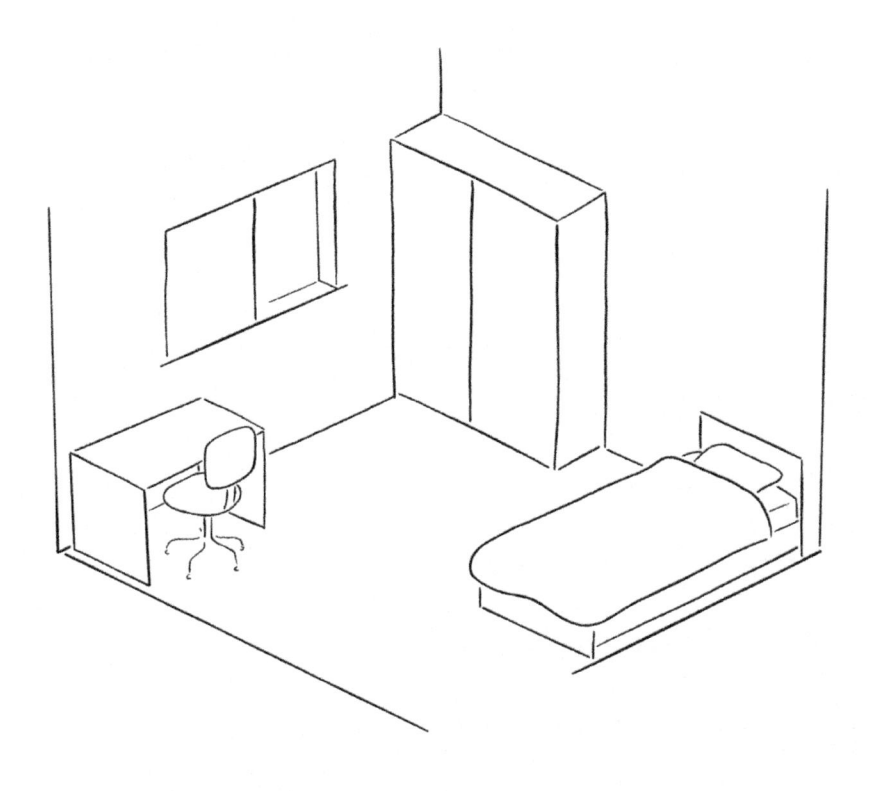

Part 78 - Declutter

Declutter.

Let go of anything that doesn't bring you joy.

Marie Kondo, a world-renowned tidying expert, has a simple way to declutter:

Hold an object or a piece of clothing in your hands.

Take a deep breath in and ask yourself:

"Does this spark joy?"

I also like to ask:

"Do I absolutely love this?"

And if the answer is a "yes", keep it.

If it's a no, thank it and let it go.

For practical items, ask yourself,

"Have I used this in the last 6-12 months?"

If you haven't, you can let it go.

If it's a sentimental item, take a photo of it before letting it go, so you can look back.

Know that the memories will always stay with you.

If the item was given to you by someone you love, you still get to keep their love minus the physical item.

When you let go of the item, you're not letting go of the love.

The love stays with you.

This might feel uncomfortable at first.

But the more you practise this, the better you will also get in letting go of people and events in life.

Then you will have more space for the new to come in.

You'll flow with life a lot more easily and effortlessly.

You'll travel through life lightly.

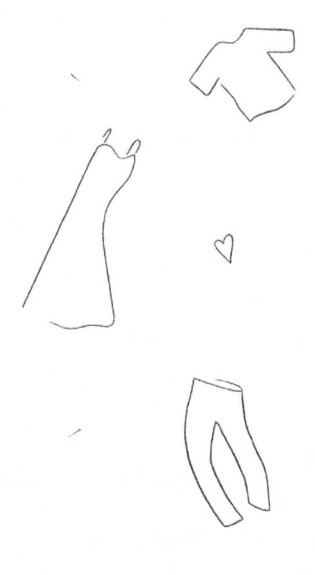

You're amazing in every way :)

Part 79 - Go To Bed Early

There is something called the circadian rhythm.

When we sleep in alignment with the sun's cycle, meaning sleeping when it gets dark, waking up when it's light, we feel so much better.

When the sun is up, our body is ready for the day.

Our mind is likely to be clearer.

Around 10pm, your body goes into cleansing the day you had physically and emotionally.

Your organs cleanse and your hormones regulate themselves.

If you're asleep during this time, you're in alignment with your body's rhythm.

To help you fall asleep easier, turn your phone off half an hour before going to bed.

This will limit your exposure to light so your body can prepare for sleep.

Try to go to bed before 10pm at night.

If you are going to bed after midnight, aim to go to bed at 12pm first.

Then aim for 11pm and then 10pm.

This will also help you get up early.

For example, if you're getting up at midday, you'll naturally start to get up at 9am.

Then at 8am.

Then at 7am.

This might feel lame at first.

Over time, you'll see that you're going to feel so much better.

Get into that rhythm.

Go to bed at similar times.

Get up at similar times.

Keep that consistency.

You're amazing in every way :)

DAYTIME

get up at 7-9 am

go to bed at 10-12 pm

NIGHT TIME

Part 80 - Allow Yourself To Rest

Sleep.

And rest.

Rest is productive.

Your brain will work so much better after.

Maybe you grew up with a parent that was restless.

They never sat down to rest.

Maybe when they saw you resting, they told you to get up and do something.

So you never learnt how to truly rest.

And do nothing.

Remind yourself that you're not them.

You can choose to rest.

Knowing you'll be so much more productive after.

You're amazing in every way :)

Part 81 - Nourish Yourself

Find out what nourishes you.

And what depletes you.

Make more time for what nourishes you.

For example, what's nourishing for me is solo time in nature.

Taking baths.

Watching a good movie.

Having a deep and real conversation with a close friend.

What depletes me is going to too many events back to back.

Being around people who aren't present and listening.

Fitting my schedule into someone else's when it goes against what I want.

So reflect on what is good for you and what isn't.

And make sure to do what's good for you regularly.

You're amazing in every way :)

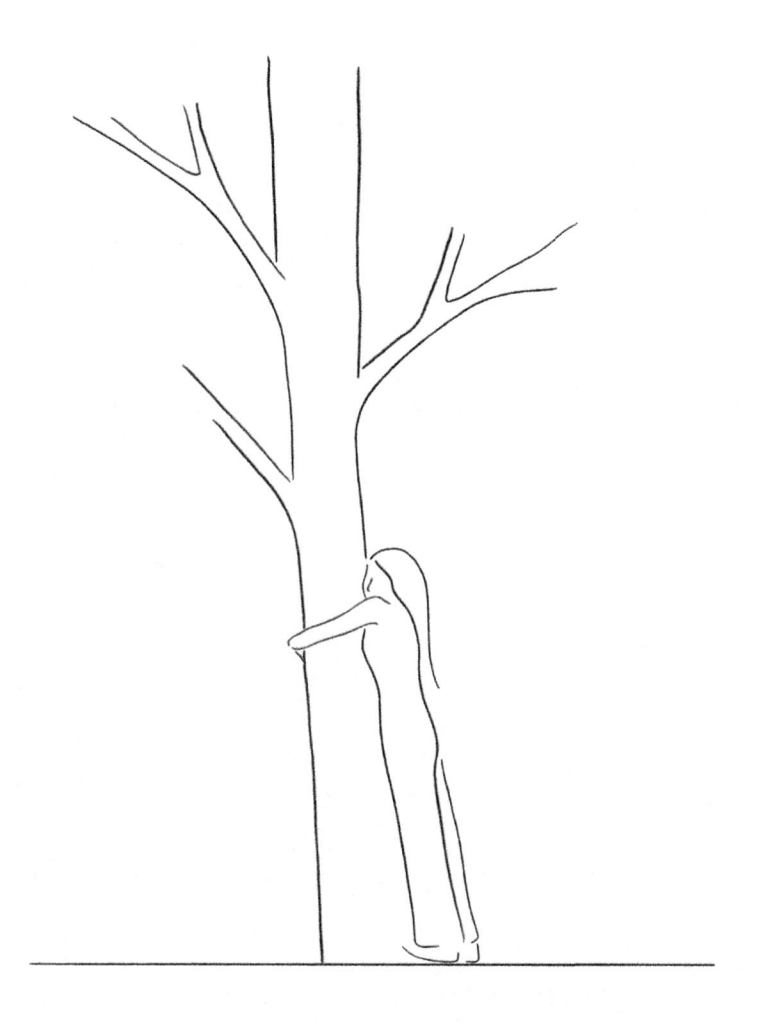

Part 82 - Nature

Nature is like home.

It's where we come from. It's where we will go.

We are nature.

When you're feeling down, go and spend time in nature.

Go somewhere lovely like a park, a forest, a river and just look around.

Notice what you can see, hear, smell, touch and even taste.

When you engage all five senses, you will start to be more present.

Lay down near the trees.

Imagine the trees holding you, grounding and hugging you.

Imagine you have roots going down to Earth, breathing in strength and grounding from there.

Let the trees remind you that you can stand tall in any storms of life.

As you sit by a river, let the river wash away anything you want to let go.

The river doesn't stop when it comes to a rock.

It finds a way to go around it or over it.

Let the river remind you to keep going in life.

As you watch the sea, let the rhythms of the waves remind you of the ebbs and flows of life.

Nothing stays the same. Even the good things.

Everything changes.

You can't capture the same wave twice.

Everything is transient.

When you're more present, you'll start to appreciate the little things in life which then add to the big things.

Nature can be a great teacher in whatever you're going through.

So go to nature and let it show you.

Listen and be present.

You're amazing in every way :)

Part 83 - Dance it Out

When you have a really bad day, put your headphones on and put on your favourite music.

Lock your door and just dance it out.

Move your body however you want to move your body.

There's no right or wrong way.

Don't try to do choreography or anything.

Dance however you're feeling in the moment.

Make some sounds, breathe and move.

You're going to feel so much better.

You're amazing in every way :)

Part 84 - Shake Your Body

When you feel anxious, move your body.

Go for a walk or put on a song you like and dance.

Moving your body will help move the energy.

You can also shake off your body.

For this, have your feet shoulder width apart.

Imagine the floor beneath you is a vibrating floor.

Bend your knees and start to shake.

Allow the shake to move all the way up from your legs to your head.

Let go of your arms, hips, back, neck and head.

This will allow you to come back to a much more grounded and peaceful place.

Do this whenever you're stressed, worried or angry.

Know that nothing is the end of the world, no matter what your mind says.

So move and shake it off.

You're amazing in every way :)

Part 85 - Morning Pages

Do your morning pages.

Morning pages are three pages of writing you do every morning, an exercise created by Julia Cameron, the author of *The Artist's Way*.

It's like a brain dump.

Imagine your mind is the sea and normally there are crazy waves there.

Morning pages allow your waters to calm down so you can notice even when a feather falls down onto the water.

You write first thing in the morning after you wake up.

You can write whatever's in your mind at that moment.

It can be about your parents, friends or school.

About anything and everything.

You can write about the day before.

You can write about the ideas you have and how you feel.

This way you're not suppressing them.

You're allowing yourself to feel everything.

You can ask questions in those pages.

You can write the answers that come.

When you're writing, don't censor it.

Write it as it is.

Be honest.

This is your secret diary.

Keep it in a place where no one can find it.

I started this practice in 2015 and kept it going.

Still to this day, I write 1-2 pages every day.

It really helps me let go of the day before, clear my mind and start the day fresh.

Give it a go.

You're amazing in every way :)

Part 86 - Let Go Of Emotions

Whenever you feel down, angry, nervous, stressed, have a notebook and just write it out.

Write out all these emotions and let them go.

Or record a voice note to yourself,

"I feel sad that.."

"I feel anxious about.."

And keep talking until you're complete.

These emotions just want to be felt.

You're amazing in every way :)

Part 87 - Little Book of Magic

Have a little notebook where you write down all the magical things that happened that day.

It may be a stranger smiling at you.

Someone complimenting you.

A friend giving you a gift for no reason.

Thinking of becoming an actor and on the same day hearing someone's success story of becoming an actor.

Write it in there.

When you feel disconnected, open up this notebook and read it.

You will remember and reconnect with magic.

And because you're writing all the magical things down, you'll start to see the magical and beautiful moments in your life more.

We find what we're looking for.

You're amazing in every way :)

Part 88 - Stay In Your Own Energy

If you're a sensitive person, you're likely to feel deeply and empathise with other people.

You might feel some emotions that they are feeling.

Here's what you can do to stay in your own energy:

When you're on your own, notice how you feel being in your own space.

Place your hands underneath your rib cage where your centre is.

Think of this as your power centre.

Remember this feeling of being in your space.

This is your energy. This is what being you feels like.

When you're about to leave the house or you're going into an environment full of people, imagine a white light bubble around you.

This bubble will protect your energy.

It won't let other people's energy go into your space.

This is especially useful when you're around people who you feel heavy around.

If you feel any unwanted energy coming your way from others, tell yourself in your mind,

"Let go".

Just imagine sending it back to where it came from.

Or imagine dropping it to the ground from the soles of your feet.

When I first started doing this, I was studying architecture. I went into the studio one day feeling energised and great. Within five minutes of sitting down, I started to feel so sleepy. I looked across and saw my friend falling asleep. As soon as I noticed that, I imagined sending that energy back.

Even just having awareness helps.

It's not that these energies are bad. It's just not your energy.

The more you practise this, it will strengthen your energetic boundaries.

You don't have to take on what's not yours.

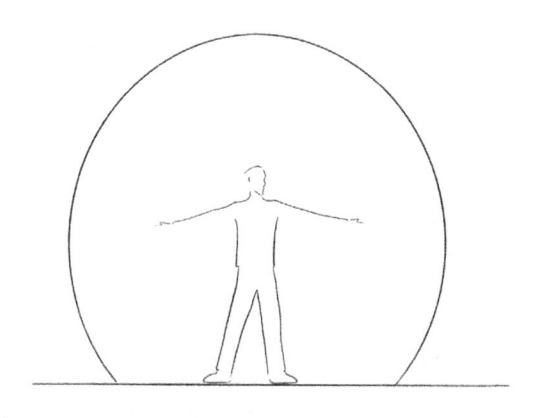

You're amazing in every way :)

BE YOURSELF

Part 89 - Be Yourself

Don't be afraid to lead.

Don't be afraid to stand out.

Don't be afraid to have a different opinion.

You're allowed to lead.

You're allowed to stand out.

You're allowed to have a different opinion.

It's what makes you, you.

Be yourself.

You don't have to be brave.

You can decide to be brave for a moment.

Then put yourself out there.

You got this!

You're amazing in every way :)

Part 90 - Different Parts

You're a complex human.

You can't be the same person all the time.

You have so many parts living in you.

You can see them as different characters living together as a crew.*

Let's say you're about to give a presentation.

You're feeling scared and nervous.

You can ask yourself,

"Which character needs to step in for this challenge?"

Maybe it's this confident and sassy girl.

Or let's say you have school work to finish.

And you're feeling overwhelmed.

You can ask yourself,

"Who needs to step in for this?"

Maybe it's this machine man focused on getting stuff done.

You have so many parts in you.

Ask for their help.

Let them guide and support you.**

Let them live.

You're amazing in every way :)

*This is inspired by my energy worker coach Todd Roache and by Internal Family Systems Therapy (IFS) also known as Parts Work, created by Dr. Richard Schwartz.

**Go to www.isiktlabar.com/guidedmeditations for the meditation to allow and connect with all your parts.

Part 91 - Who You Are

No one can define who you are.

Just because someone tells you mean things, shouts at you or tells you things that make you feel like crap, it doesn't mean you're these things.

It says more about who they are than who you are.

Don't pay attention to them.

No person, no event, not anything can take you away from who you truly are.

You're amazing in every way :)

Part 92 - You're Unique

Don't be afraid to be different.

Don't compromise on who you are in order to receive love.

There will be friends who want to hang out with you for who you are.

Choose the people that make you feel good about yourself.

Not the opposite.

Don't compare yourself with others.

Everyone has their own journey.

No one has the experiences that you had.

No one has the ideas that you have.

You're unique in your own way.*

Someone else is unique in their own way.

Focus on you, your truth and your life.

If you're going to use comparison, compare yourself with who you used to be.

Not with someone else.

You're amazing in every way :)

*Go to www.isiktlabar.com/guidedmeditations for the
meditation to connect with your true nature.

Part 93 - Create Your Own Style

Wear the clothes you want to wear.

Style your hair how you want to style it.

Don't worry about what your friends and family say.

It is your self-expression.

Wear the clothes that you feel good in.

Do your hair however it makes you feel more like you.

If you love it, that's all that matters.

And you can always change your mind.

Have fun with it.

You're amazing in every way :)

Part 94 - Focus On Your Surroundings

You might not know what to do with your arms when you're walking.

You might feel like everyone's watching you.

You might feel self-conscious as you're walking or talking.

You're not the only one feeling this way.

There are many others feeling this worry too.

So, if everyone's worrying about this, no one is actually doing the watching.

Everyone's worrying about how they're looking from the outside.

Instead of focusing on yourself, put your attention outwards.

Focus on your surroundings.

Focus on your friends or the situation you're in.

The more you focus on something that's not working, it's going to carry on not working.

It will also make you feel more self-conscious about it.

Focus on where you want to go and what's working.

You're amazing in every way :)

Part 95 - You Don't Have To Be Perfect

You don't have to be perfect to be loved.

You're loveable as you are.

Your imperfections are what make you human.

Everything about you, including the things you might not like, makes you, you.

Embrace everything that you are, including your flaws.

They're beautiful.

Don't put so much pressure on yourself to be perfect.

Or to get things right.

Embrace your imperfections.

You're amazing in every way :)

Part 96 - Your Worth Is Not Based On What You Do

Sometimes you might feel guilty for not being productive.

Remember you're a human being.

You're not a human doing.

You don't always have to do things.

You can relax and do nothing.

Your worth doesn't come from doing things.

It comes from who you are.

If you didn't complete the things you wanted to do today, that's okay.

Don't be so hard on yourself.

Nothing is lost. Nothing is ruined.

It doesn't mean anything about you.

You're still loved. You're still capable.

You still have it all in you.

You can try again tomorrow.

You're amazing in every way :)

Part 97 - Share Yourself

What you have to share matters.

If you want to share something, do it.

If you want to say something in class, but you're feeling shy, put your hand up and share it.

If you want to say something amongst your friends, but you're feeling worried they'll judge you, share it anyway.

Your opinion matters.

You're intelligent.

You're creative.

You have a lot to offer.

You matter.

When you don't share yourself, you're robbing the world of your magnificence.

You're amazing in every way :)

Part 98 - Take Up Space

It's important to say sorry when you hurt someone.

But don't be sorry for existing.

For walking.

For breathing.

And for being who you are.

Take up space.

Own who you are.

As girls, we're often taught to be good girls.

We're taught to not rock the boat.

We're taught to do as we're told.

This might lead to making ourselves smaller.

We might shrink ourselves.

Notice when you do this.

And allow yourself to be big instead.

Be proud of who you are.

You're amazing in every way :)

Part 99 - Confidence

Don't focus on trying to be confident.

It actually doesn't matter.

The more you know yourself, the more confident you'll be.

And the more you'll embrace everything that you are.

Real confidence comes from knowing yourself.

Instead of trying to be confident, let go of what others think of you.

Their opinions don't matter.

Discover who you are.

Explore this vast and limitless world inside of you.

When you're at peace with all that's inside of you, you won't care as much about what the outside says.

You're amazing in every way :)

Part 100 - You Know

Stop saying "I don't know."

Every time you tell yourself that you don't know, you're reinforcing the belief that you don't know.

It makes you lose trust in yourself.

Instead, ask yourself:

"What if I did know?"

"What would that look like?"

"How would that be?"

"What would someone who knows do?"

That starts to turn the "I don't know" to "Maybe I do know".

It doesn't even matter what decision you make in that space.

What matters is that you make a decision and act on it.

You can always adjust later.

You're amazing in every way :)

Part 101 - Make Your Own Choices

Your life will be shaped by the collection of the choices you'll make.

You can ask your friends, family or others for their opinion.

But when it comes to having the final say in the decision, always go with what feels right for you.

With every decision you make, your life will contract or expand.

Your life will be filled with either what you love or a compromise.

Choose what you love.

You don't ever have to compromise.

You're amazing in every way :)

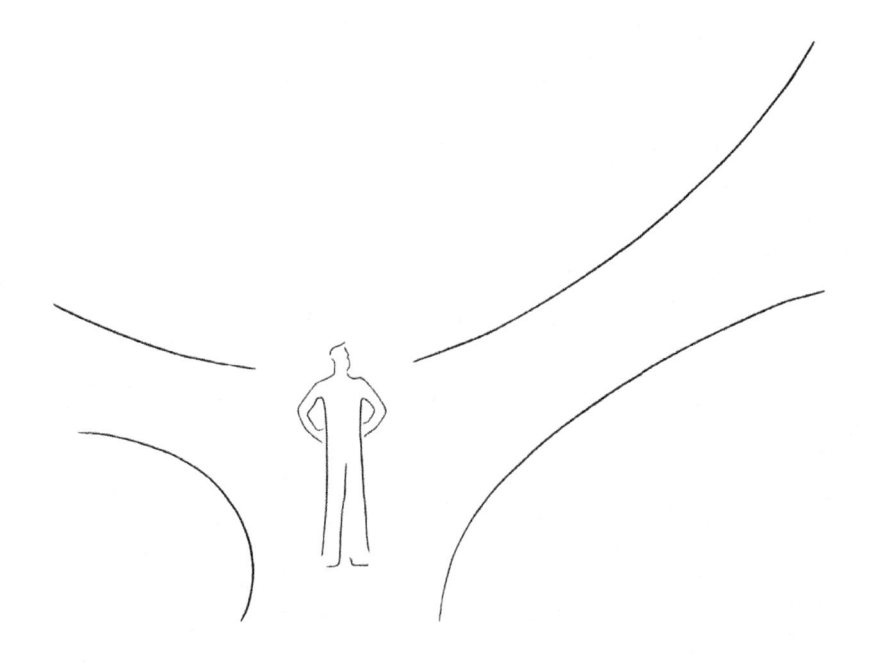

Part 102 - We're All Equal

You're not worse or better than anyone.

You're equal to everyone.

You might feel everyone is better than you.

This might make you feel small.

You might hand over your power to others.

Or you might feel that you're better than everyone.

This can make you feel superior or egotistical.

It might lead you to separate yourself from everyone and feel lonely.

We have our differences and similarities.

But we're all equal.

So ask yourself:

"If I knew I was equal to everyone, what would I say? What would I do? And how would I show up?"

And follow that.

You're amazing in every way :)

*we are different
yet the same*

Part 103 - Ask For Help

Asking for help doesn't make you weak.

Quite the opposite, it makes you stronger.

It allows people to give you love and support.

People who care about you would love to do this for you.

So it's a win-win.

Don't shy away from asking for help.

Don't rob them of the honour of being there for you.

We're not meant to do life on our own.

Ask for help when you need it.

You're amazing in every way :)

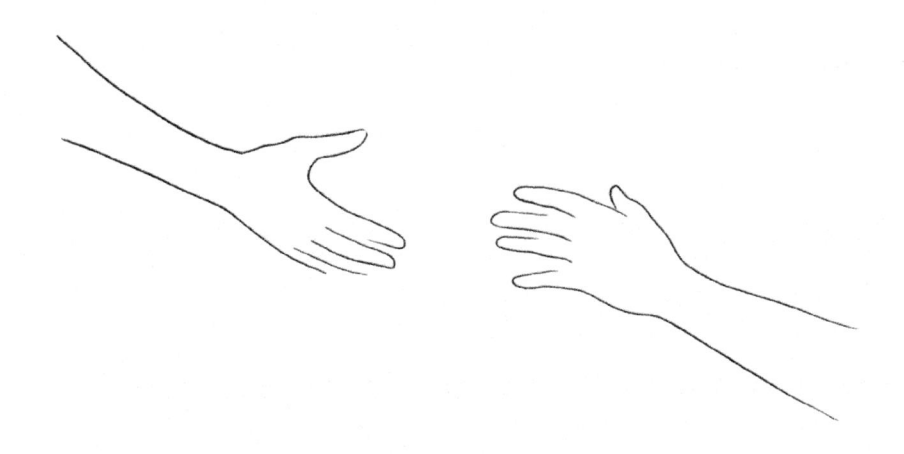

Part 104 - Allow Change

You don't have to be the same person all the time.

Your interests might change.

Your hobbies might change.

What you're into might change.

And that's ok.

It's natural.

Allow yourself to change.

It shows that you're evolving.

That you're growing.

The only constant in life is change.

Don't worry about what people around you might say.

Keep being yourself.

Even if it means being a different person to who you were yesterday.

You're amazing in every way :)

Part 105 - Put Yourself In The Right Environment

A flower blooms when it has the right conditions.

These are sunlight, water and the minerals from the soil.

You're like that.

Imagine you're a flower.

In order to bloom, you need to be in the right environment.

Maybe that's to go out in nature, work out or to journal.

Or it's doing what you love.

Or hanging out with friends you love and feel loved by.

So ask yourself,

"If I were a flower, what conditions would I need to bloom and shine?

And follow that.

Make sure your environment allows you to bloom.

You're amazing in every way :)

Part 106 - You Will Become

You don't need to have all the answers right now.

And that's ok.

An acorn doesn't have to figure out how to become an oak tree.

There's an intelligence that lies within the acorn that will allow it to become an oak tree.

It just becomes.

You'll become.

You're amazing in every way :)

Part 107 - Allow Yourself To Evolve

Our true nature naturally grows and creates.

When we put ourselves in a box, we're limiting this change and evolution.

When you get out of the box,

Out of the lines,

Out of the conditioning,

Out of the rules you were taught,

There's all this space you can explore and play in.

In that space, there are no limits to what you can be and do.

Allow yourself to evolve.

Allow yourself to become.

Be curious and open.

Express yourself.

You're amazing in every way :)

Q&A 1

"I have a sister that judges me for everything I do and it makes me very angry and sad at the same time. I don't know what to do."

Whenever someone judges you, it likely has nothing to do with you.

They might be judging themselves.

The way someone treats you often shows how they treat themselves.

I know it's hard.

I know it's making you feel sad and angry.

Know that they can't take away from who you truly are.

Whenever they judge you, take a deep breath in.

Imagine everything they say washing over you like water.

Just let it pass through you.

And keep being yourself.

You're amazing in every way :)

Q&A 2

"I'm really scared to get a short haircut bcs i never had short hair but i have no idea how i would look and i really want to get a short haircut"

If you really want to get a shorter haircut and you're 100% sure, then go for it.

I had long curly hair most of my life.

Then I cut my hair really short when I was 16.

I loved it at the time.

It took me years to grow it again.

Then I shaved my hair again on my 30th birthday.

I turned it into a ritual.

I asked 12 of my close friends to sit in a circle around me as I shaved my head.

Then one by one, they came up to me and looked into my eyes lovingly.

They all hugged me in the end.

It felt like a rebirth.

It was one of the most powerful and loving rituals I held for myself.

Now my hair is super short.

I absolutely love it.

It feels like me.

And recently, I decided to grow it again.

I'm not saying shave your head.

But what I'm saying is, if there's a part of you that wants to cut your hair shorter, then you can do that.

Every time you have a different haircut or hair style, you get to express a different part of yourself.

It can be creative and fun.

If you don't like it, you can always grow your hair back.

You're amazing in every way :)

Q&A 3

"I want to become an actor but I have no idea how to start and I feel like I would be really awkward and quiet? Do you have any advice?"

You can be shy and still be successful.

You can be awkward and still create amazing things.

Being quiet, shy and awkward is not everything that you are.

There are other parts of you.

The chapters in this book were made from TikTok videos.

At times, I felt weird and awkward making these videos looking into the camera.

But what I love is helping you all.

I loved seeing the comments saying how much the videos helped you.

I loved seeing the questions that formed some of these chapters.

I made that more important than being awkward and shy.

The part of me that loves helping became stronger than the part of me that felt shy or weird.

Beyoncé has an alter ego, meaning a part of her called Sasha Fierce.

She steps onto the stage not as herself, but as Sasha Fierce.

You can do the same.

Create a Confident Self, even give her a name.

You can also give your Shy Self a name.

Love them both.

They're both parts of you.

If I can do it, you can do it too.

You're amazing in every way :)

DREAMS

Part 108 - Your Dreams Are Powerful

If you have a dream, you also have what it takes to create it.

If you're asking yourself,

"Would I love to do it?"

And you're getting a "yes", just do it!

Don't even question it.

Don't worry if you don't feel good enough.

If you don't feel worthy.

Or if you don't feel confident.

None of that matters.

Trying to feel good enough, worthy, confident or trying to fix yourself in any way first, can actually be a distraction from going for your dreams.

What matters is that it excites you.

That you'd love to do it.

Your dreams are never random.

Trust that they are put in your heart for a reason.

You have all the imagination, creativity, power and resources to make it real.

One of my favourite quotes is by Richard Bach, author of *Jonathan Livingston Seagull,* saying,

"You are never given a dream without also being given the power to make it true."

You don't need confidence.

You don't have to feel good enough or confident.

You just need the desire to go for it.

Believe in yourself.

You can do anything you put your mind to.

You're amazing in every way :)

Part 109 - Ego vs Soul

When you're moving towards your dream, it's important to know the difference between your Ego and your Soul.

Your Ego is your survival mechanism.

This is where your unconscious beliefs lie, keeping you safe, small and secure.

It's your limited self where you repeat the past.

Living from your Ego is like living in fear.

It's your False Self.

It communicates to you through your thoughts and feelings.

Your Soul is your higher self, your greatness and your limitless self.

This is where your gifts lie.

It's the part of you that is connected to everything through all space and time.

It gives you inspired perspectives and expands your possibilities.

It's your limitless self that allows you to expand, evolve and grow.

Living from your Soul is like living in love.

It's your True Self.

It communicates to you through your intuition.

When you act from your Ego, you create more Ego.

When you act from Soul, you create more Soul.

Your Ego can often get in the way of listening to your intuition.

Next time you're about to make a decision, ask yourself:

"What would my Soul say? How would my Soul do?"

And follow that.

You're amazing in every way :)

Part 110 - Own Your Dreams

Never give up on your dreams.

Steven Spielberg, the director of *E.T*, *Jurassic Park*, *Ready Player One* and *The Terminal* said,

"The hardest thing to listen to - your instincts, your human personal intuition - always whispers; it never shouts. Very hard to hear. So you have to every day of your lives be ready to hear what whispers in your ear; it very rarely shouts."

If you're hearing the whisper telling you to follow your dream, pay attention to the whisper.

Instead of listening to the doubts, fears and worries, pay attention to the whisper.

Act on what it's telling you to do.

These are your precious dreams.

Own them.

You're amazing in every way :)

Part 111 - Discover Your Dreams

It's completely ok to not know what your dreams are.

You might be reading this chapter and thinking,

"What if I don't actually have any dreams?"

Then try new things.

Experiment and explore.

You're not alone in this.

You have your whole life ahead of you to find out what your passions and dreams are.

As you're trying new things, ask yourself:

"Am I enjoying this? Do I love doing this? Does this excite me? Would I like to do this again?"

If you get excited about something, that's a good sign that it could be for you.

Enthusiasm should be your North Star.

If you aren't enthusiastic, let it go.

Move onto the next thing.

Don't let it mean anything about you or your life.

Give yourself permission to try new things.

To make mistakes.

To adjust.

And then keep going.

Sooner or later, you will find something you feel enthusiastic about.

It's inevitable.

And there is no rush.

You're amazing in every way :)

Part 112 - Listen To Your Intuition

Your intuition is like your best friend guiding you to your dreams.

It knows what lights you up.

It's like your navigation system in life guiding you towards your dream life.

It gives you the next steps to follow your highest truth.

Make sure to act on its guidance.

Listening to your intuition is like a muscle you grow.

The more you listen, the more you can hear it.

Think of it like a friend who is asking you to meet and you keep saying no.

They will stop asking after a while.

So ask yourself, "What's my intuition telling me?"

And follow through on that to come closer to your heart and your highest truth.

You're amazing in every way :)

Part 113 - Connect To The Magic Of Life

Our minds receive so much information at any moment.

We are only aware of what our Ego believes is needed in order to survive.

This keeps you in survival mode instead of thriving.

Einstein said,

"We cannot solve our problems with the same level of thinking that created them."

You have to rise above to another level.

You can do this by accessing a state called Innocence.

Innocence is a state of awe and wonder outside of your thoughts and feelings.

Here, you let go of the need to know.

It's where you open up to the magic of life.

Where you're free of judgements.

Where you let go of assumptions and expectations.

Where you get to experience life as a clean slate.

Look at a baby or a 3-4 year old toddler.

Or imagine yourself when you were 4 years old.

They take everything in as new information.

For them, every moment is a new moment.

Here's how you can go into innocence:

Close your eyes.

Take three or four deep breaths.

Relax your jaw, shoulders and belly.

Now imagine a golden ball of light above your head that represents innocence.

It descends down onto your head.

As soon as it touches your head, it lights up your whole body.

You're in innocence, free and empty.

You're connected through all space and time.

You can also imagine looking at the world from the eyes of a child.

In curiosity, awe and wonder.

Look at the person in front of you, as if it's the first time you're seeing them.

Look at the trees, sea, sky as if it's the first time you're seeing them.

What do you notice that you didn't notice before?

Even when you're looking at something you've seen before.

Look for what you haven't seen.

Set the intention to open yourself up to magic.

This will make magic more available to you.

When you're living in a way that's more connected with magic, your intuition will also grow stronger.

Practising being in innocence is one of the fastest and easiest ways to connect to magic.

You can listen to the guided meditation*.

This is best to do in nature.

After you've listened to the meditation, look around and notice everything.

You can even walk around in innocence and see where you're drawn to.

Take in your surroundings without checking your phone.

You'll have a deeper presence, heightened sense of awareness, gratitude for life, clarity and connection to magic.

You're amazing in every way :)

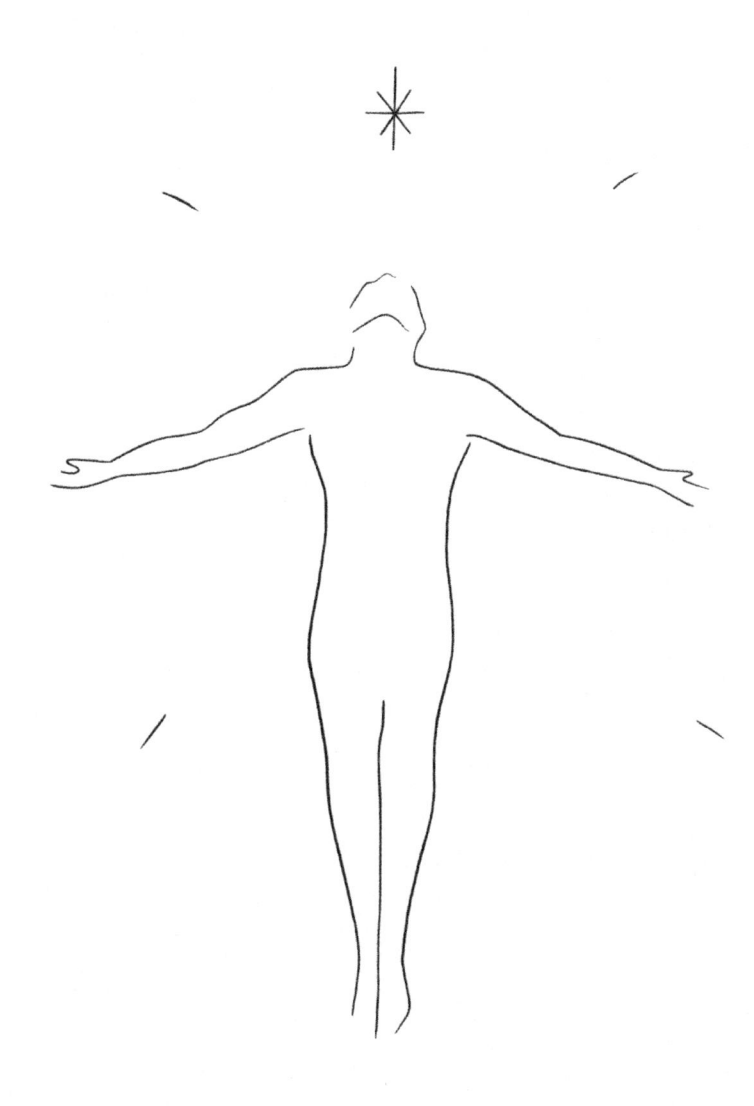

*Go to www.isiktlabar.com/guidedmeditations for the meditation to connect with innocence.

Part 114 - Connect With Your Truth

You always have your highest truth.

Or the best potential outcome in every situation.

This is the most aligned choice.

Every choice you make will lead you to a different pathway.

If the choice you're making is more aligned with your truth, the path will be more aligned as well.

Follow the truth that will give you the most happiness and fulfilment.

Here's how to connect with your truth:

First acknowledge your Ego around the topic you're looking into.

Notice what you're telling yourself.

Notice how you're feeling about it.

Notice what these thoughts and feelings are telling you to do or not do.

Then close your eyes.

Imagine rising above the situation.

You're looking at it from a higher perspective.

Now imagine a golden ball of light above your head.

It descends down onto your body.

As soon as it touches your head, you're free and empty of everything.

You're in innocence.

You're connected to everything through all space and time.

Then ask your question:

"What would I love?"

"What's my truth?"

"What's really going on?"

Then ask,

"What's the emotion of what I'd love?"

Maybe it's love, connection, freedom etc.

Ask,

"What's that telling me to do or not do?"

Trust what you get and follow that.*

When you follow it, you start to bring the highest and most aligned pathway into reality.

You're amazing in every way :)

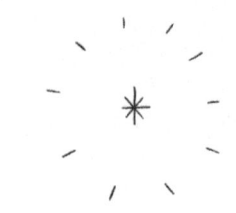

connect with innocence

what would I love

follow the next step

*Go to www.isiktlabar.com/guidedmeditations for the meditation to rise above your thoughts and feelings and connect with your truth.

Part 115 - Egoic And True Vision

When you're going towards creating your dreams, there are two concepts to be aware:

Egoic and true vision.

Egoic vision comes from the opposite of what you don't want.

It's driven by a push to get away from something.

It comes from fear.

True vision is what you truly want for the sake of it.

It's driven by a pull towards your dream.

It comes from love.

Let's say you want to be in a relationship because you feel lonely.

That's an egoic vision.

The true vision would be wanting to be in a relationship because you want to share love, go on adventures with someone or be in a loving sacred union.

There are no other agendas.

Another egoic vision would be wanting to stop eating unhealthy food.

A true vision would be being healthy.

This not only covers stopping eating unhealthy food, it covers sleeping well, exercising, eating well, etc.

It comes with an overall sense of well-being.

It comes from a higher vibration.

True vision comes from what truly brings you alive, brings you joy and fills you up.

Ask yourself,

"Where is this coming from? Is it from my Ego or my Soul?"

Turn the egoic vision into a true one.

Even if the action you take is the same, the energy behind it will be different.

That will make a huge difference.

You're amazing in every way :)

Part 116 - Trust Yourself

Trust yourself.

Trust what you think is best for you.

No one has the right answer, but you.

Close your eyes.

Take a few deep breaths and ask yourself,

 "What do I want?"

Whatever you get, follow that.

Take action on that.

The more you listen to your intuition and act on it, the louder it will speak to you.

And the more your trust in yourself and your intuition, it will grow.

You're amazing in every way :)

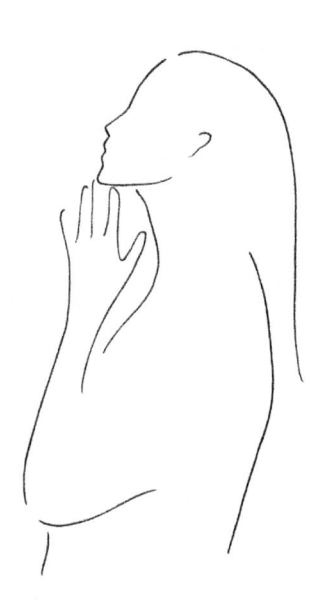

Part 117 - You Can Do Anything

You're powerful beyond belief.

You can do anything you put your mind to.

If you want to do something, go and do it.

So give yourself permission to do what you love.

You're amazing in every way :)

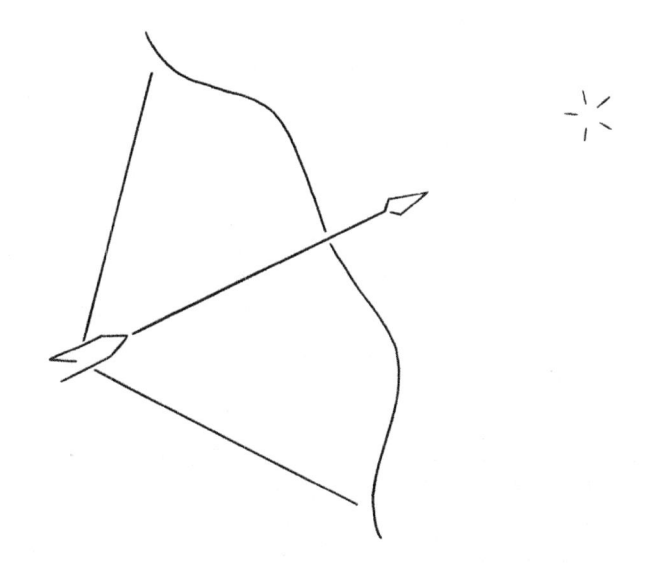

Part 118 - Conscious Creation

We're creative beings and we're always creating.

We either create drama or our dreams.

We either create from our Ego or from our Soul.

We either create from fear or from love.

We get to choose.

Unchanneled creative energy turns into destructive energy.

We almost have to consciously choose to create.

Otherwise we will go into destructive energy.

We need to have a focus on a vision.

When we're going for what our hearts want, our Ego might sneak in and try to sabotage.

Whenever creative energy builds, we resolve it unconsciously through self-sabotage.

When we know what we're doing, then we have a choice to change it.

Here are some examples of self-sabotage:

Blaming others.

Convincing yourself you didn't want it anyway.

Sulking.

Giving up.

Procrastinating.

Doing unimportant tasks to keep yourself busy so you never get around to doing what you wanted to do.

Asking other people's opinion and trusting that over yours.

Overthinking or over researching.

Having a backup plan if all else fails.

Celebrating early before you actually created the thing.

Numbing yourself with food.

Shopping.

We all do a form of these.

Notice when you're coming from self-sabotage.

Take your focus back into the vision and ask, "What would I love?"*

Act on that.

You're amazing in every way :)

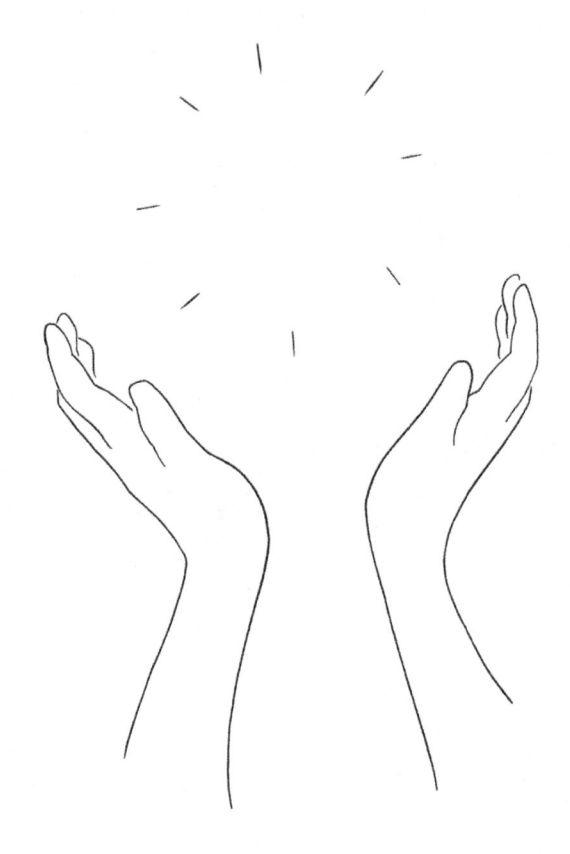

*I learnt the intuitive work on how to create what we love from two of my teachers William Whitecloud, the author of *The Magician's Way, Secrets to Natural Success* and Ryan Pinnick, CEO of *SuperGenius*.

Part 119 - Masculine And Feminine In Creation

No matter what gender we are, we all have both masculine and feminine energy within us.

Feminine energy is inward energy which is yin.

Masculine energy is outward energy which is yang.

When you receive the idea that is yin.

Then you take action, that is yang.

The final step is to surrender and let go.

You allow the creation to come to life which is yin.

You repeat this cycle.

If you're always receiving ideas but not taking action, it's an excess of yin.

All that built up energy can implode and create anxiety.

If you're always taking action, but not surrendering, letting it come to you, it's an excess of yang.

This can create burnout.

So creating is like a partnered dance between the yin and yang.

If you're waiting for the other person to take all the steps, you're quite passive.

If you're taking all the steps and not listening to your partner, you're quite active.

A beautiful harmonious dance is when you both flow between each other.

Just like a balanced dialogue where two sides are equally sharing and listening.

Keep dancing between both energies.*

And have fun in your process of creating.

You're amazing in every way :)

▽

receive the idea

+

△

take action

+

▽

surrender

=

✳

idea created

*Go to www.isiktlabar.com/guidedmeditations for the meditation to bring harmony between your masculine and feminine.

Part 120 - Trust Your Timing

You have time.

You have all the time in the world.

You might be feeling worried that you won't have time to do all the things you want to do.

You will.

You have your whole life in front of you.

You have all the time to explore.

You have all the time to create.

You have all the time to love and be loved.

You have all the time to be you.

You have all the time to make mistakes.

You have all the time to learn.

You're just getting started.

Trust your timing.

You're amazing in every way :)

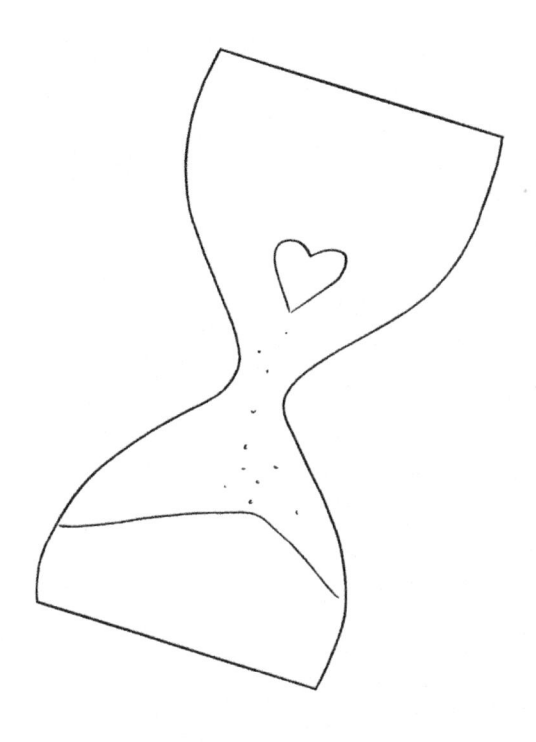

Part 121 - Follow Your Dream

Go for your dream.

If you have something in your heart that makes you feel alive, follow that.

That's where your magic is.

It's ok to feel as though you're not good enough.

To feel unworthy.

To feel like you don't have what it takes.

To feel scared of disappointing your family.

To feel worried that others might judge you.

Or whatever it might be.

They're all stories.

And they're not true.

The truth is that when you follow your dreams, a higher and truer part of you comes alive.

Your Soul.

You start to become the person in your dreams.

Your Soul and the universe, God, a higher power, whatever you want to call it, starts to work together to bring your dreams to reality.

All it takes is for you to say "yes" to it.

Believe it and follow it.

You're amazing in every way :)

Part 122 - Write Your Dreams

Having a powerful vision is super important in keeping you focused towards your dreams.

If you're feeling stuck, lost or just feeling in a lower vibration, there's a chance that you haven't used your intuition and imagination to create a powerful vision.

Or you haven't connected to your dreams.

Get your notebook and pen.

Set aside 25 minutes for this exercise.

You will be connecting with your dream life and writing down any dreams you might have about anything.

This is the dream life you want to live.

If anything was possible, it's the way you would choose to live.

In the first part, you'll be writing down your visions for 20 minutes.

In the second part, you'll receive your next intuitive action.

When you're connecting with your intuition to receive your next steps, you'll often get the very next step.

You won't get the whole 10 year plan.

As you take action and keep asking, you'll get the following steps.

Let's begin with the first part:

Close your eyes, take a deep breath.

Set the intention to connect with your dream life vision.

Choose to receive it easily and effortlessly.

Imagine now you're in a forest surrounded by trees.

See all the colours around you.

Notice what you can see and hear.

Maybe you can hear the birds singing.

Notice the aliveness around you.

You start to walk in this forest and with every step, you're going deeper and deeper into yourself.

You can feel your awareness is getting more heightened.

Even the colours around you are brighter.

The sounds are louder.

You then walk into a clearing that is surrounded by a circle of trees.

This space almost has a sacred feeling about it.

You walk to the centre of it.

Now imagine a golden circle in front of you.

This circle represents the vision of your dream life.

It's there.

And it's already created on some level in it's full potential.

When you're ready, step in and become one with the energy of this circle.

Notice what you can see.

Notice how it feels in your body.

Receive what's in your heart.

Maybe you want to become an actor.

Maybe you want to travel.

Maybe you want to write books.

Write it all down in the present tense.

Imagine as you're writing it down that you're in it.

You're living it.

You're creating it.

It's happening at that moment.

Just keep writing down what it feels and looks like.

Get creative.

Use your imagination.

Let go of what you think you want.

Don't worry about how it's going to come to life.

Let go of the how.

Focus on the what for now.

And write it all down for 20 minutes.

Keep writing.

As you're writing, allow the full flourishment of it.

Ask,

"What else is there?"

Sometimes you might feel it's finished and there's nothing more to write at the 10th minute.

Keep writing.

Sometimes you get the gold in the last two minutes.

Ask,

"What am I resisting seeing?"

Keep writing until the time is up.

After you've done this, do the second part.

In the second part:

Step back into the vision circle.

Receive all the things you felt before.

Maybe you saw, heard, felt or you just knew.

As you're in the vision circle, look back at where you used to be, which is today.

This might include stories, beliefs you might be telling yourself or current situations stopping you from creating it.

Imagine a bridge coming out from there, connecting to the vision circle you're in.

Having already created it, ask yourself,

"What's my next step?"

Write down what you get.

You might get a few steps too.

Take action on those next steps.

You got it from the version of you that has created it.

That's a message from your intuition.

It's the fastest and most effortless route to your dreams.

Connect with the vision.

Ask the next step.

Take the intuitive action.

Repeat this cycle until your dreams become your reality.*

You're amazing in every way :)

*Go to www.isiktlabar.com/guidedmeditations for the meditation to write your monthly visioning. You can do this at the beginning of every month to connect with your dreams.

Part 123 - Believe In Your Dreams

When you have a dream, you're going to have two voices inside of you.

One voice that has faith.

One voice that has doubts.

You can talk to these voices.

You can ask the doubt:

"Hey, I'm listening. What do you want to share?"

It might tell you its fears and worries,

"Who do you think you are? You can't do that. You're not good enough. You're too young. Your parents wouldn't approve."

Listen.

Then respond,

"Cool, thanks for sharing."

Acknowledge it.

Don't let that voice override and impact you.

Then ask the voice that has faith.

The part of you that believes that it is possible:

"Now I'm listening to you. What do you want to share?"

And listen.

This part might say,

"I'd love to do this. This is my passion. This is what I love. You got this. You can do it."

Now you have a choice.

You can choose the one you want to act on.

The one that you want to give more energy and power to.

The fear might never go away.

And that's okay.

You can be scared and do incredible things.

You have a part in you who believes in you.

This voice is resilient.

It believes and keeps going.

Choose to listen to that part.

And act on that part.

You're amazing in every way :)

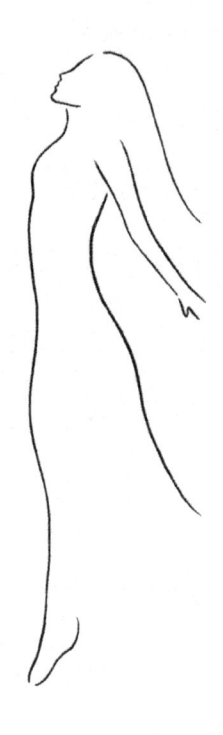

Part 124 - Receive Guidance From Your Higher Self

Your higher self is your full potential embodiment.

Everything you have ever wanted to do, be, have; this person has done it and has it.

They know you better than anyone. They've been there.

Close your eyes and imagine them.*

How do they look? How do they feel?

Now write a letter to your higher self.

Share all your concerns and worries you might have about your dreams.

Then ask any questions you might have.

Hear if there's any messages they'd like to share with you.

As Katherine Woodward Thomas suggests in her book, *Calling in "The One"*, end your letter with,

"Please write through my pen. Thank you very much."

Then write a letter back to yourself from your higher self.

Do this as many times as you like.

You're amazing in every way :)

*Go to www.isiktlabar.com/guidedmeditations for the meditation to receive guidance from your higher (future) self.

Part 125 - One Step At A Time

When you're young, your dreams may feel so big to achieve.

So how do you achieve your dreams?

You take it one step at a time.

Anyone who had a big dream took it one step at a time.

Know that you have so many years ahead of you.

Keep focusing on your dream.

And keep going.

You have time.

You're amazing in every way :)

Part 126 - Feel Inspired By Others

Don't compare yourself with others.

When you look at someone who created something amazing, you're only seeing the end result.

You don't see how much they doubted themselves.

You don't see how many times they wanted to stop.

You don't see the struggle they went through.

You only see the successful outcome.

Because they kept going.

And they created what they dreamt of creating.

So next time you look at others who have succeeded, remember:

They also had fears.

They also doubted themselves.

They're also human.

They might not share it.

They might not look like they experience those things.

But they do.

It took them years to get to the point where they are now.

So look at these people not to compare yourself.

But to inspire yourself to create your own version of success.

And remember, everyone was once a beginner who just kept going.

You're amazing in every way :)

Part 127 - Fear Of Failure

Sometimes fear of failure can stop us from going for our dreams.

We might never even begin.

You might have a dream that you're not following.

Because you might be feeling scared of failure.

If you don't try, you'll automatically fail.

It's better to fail while you're going for your dream than never trying.

The day you stop trying is the day you fail.

If you keep going, sooner or later, you'll get there.

You're amazing in every way :)

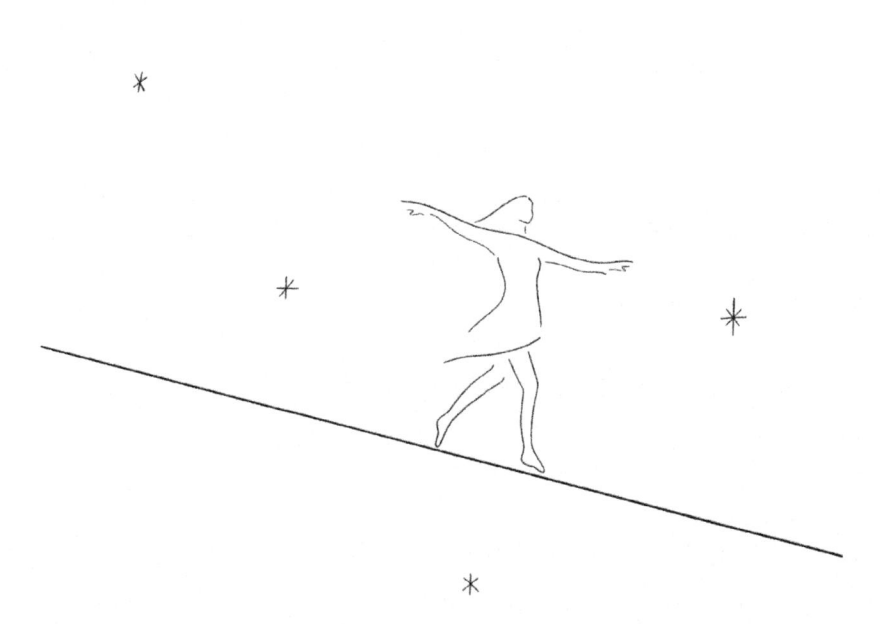

Part 128 - You're Not Too Young

You're not too young for any dream.

Age doesn't mean anything.

It's just a number.

Imagine life is a video game.

Some people get to level 30 in 30 years.

Some people get to level 30 in 5 years.

They're just levels to pass.

Not ages to become.

Just because someone is young, doesn't mean they're not wise.

People might be telling you,

"You're only 14. You're too young to know".

Don't listen to them.

Trust and stand up for your dreams.

Believe in your ideas.

You have a lot to offer.

Know that you're never too young to start anything.
You're never too old either.

If you have a dream in your heart, go for it.

You're amazing in every way :)

Part 129 - Decide And Act

You can be shy and you can do brave things.

All it takes is a decision and action.

Steve Chandler wrote in his book, *100 Ways To Motivate Yourself*, that as a boy, he once threw his hat over a wall so that he would have to climb it to get it.

If you want to do something, put yourself in a situation where you have to do it.

I led a running group during my time at university in the UK.

The group was called "Action is Life".

I used to struggle getting up at 6am for early morning runs.

So I asked who needed a wake up call in the morning.

I would call my friends up at 6am, to go for a run at 6:30am.

Because I felt responsible, I would wake up to call them.

I resisted each run.

I felt great after each run.

So many people benefitted from this group, especially during stressful study times.

You grow and evolve when you're outside of your comfort zone. Even if it feels hard.

Even if it feels uncomfortable.

Even if it feels scary.

Growth is the distance between where you are and where you want to be.

There's magic on the other side of your resistance.

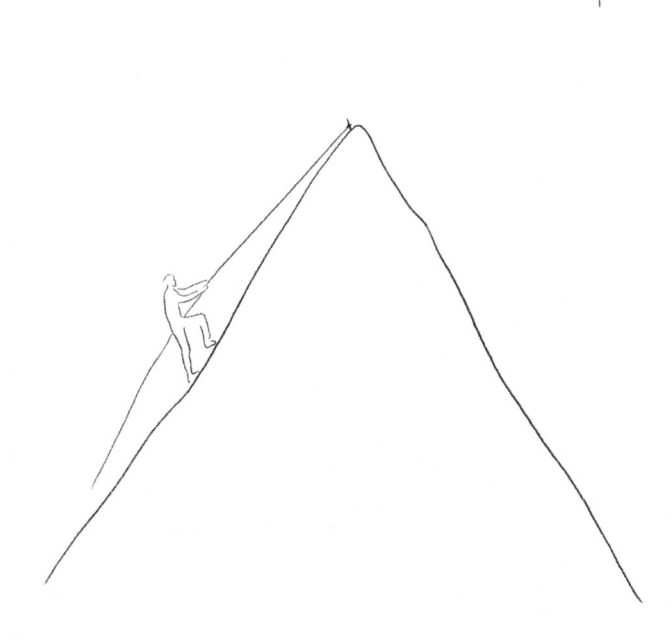

You're amazing in every way :)

Part 130 - Do Your Best

When you do something, give it your best.

Give your 100%.

If it works out, you can be proud of your achievement.

If it doesn't work out, you know you've given everything that you can.

There was nothing else you could have done.

There weren't any "what if"s.

This way, you won't have any regrets.

You'll be living free from the past feeling at peace with yourself when you go to bed.

This is the key to freedom.

Give it your all.

And have no regrets.

You're amazing in every way :)

Part 131 - Keep Going Towards Your Dreams

Sometimes we might feel disheartened by what others tell us.

Especially if it's about our dreams.

It can feel disappointing.

We might even want to give up.

Don't give up on your dreams because of something your teachers, parents or friends said.

No one can tell you what you can do.

Or cannot do.

If your teacher is inspiring, uplifting and truly believes in you, listen to them.

If someone is pessimistic, telling you that you can't realise your dreams because you're not good enough, you don't have the talent or whatever it might be, don't listen to them.

They have no idea what you're capable of.

If people are making fun of your dreams, don't pay any attention to it.

Imagine not going for your dream, because some people made fun of it.

So you waste a whole lifetime doing something you don't want to do so that people won't laugh at you.

That is a waste of your precious time and energy.

Anyone who's making fun of you because you're going for your dreams, probably hasn't gone for their own dreams.

Often people who want to bring you down were brought down by others.

Don't let their own fears and insecurities affect you.

Anyone who's going for their dreams, would support you going for your dreams.

Because they know what it takes.

So go for it!

Follow your dreams no matter what everyone else says.

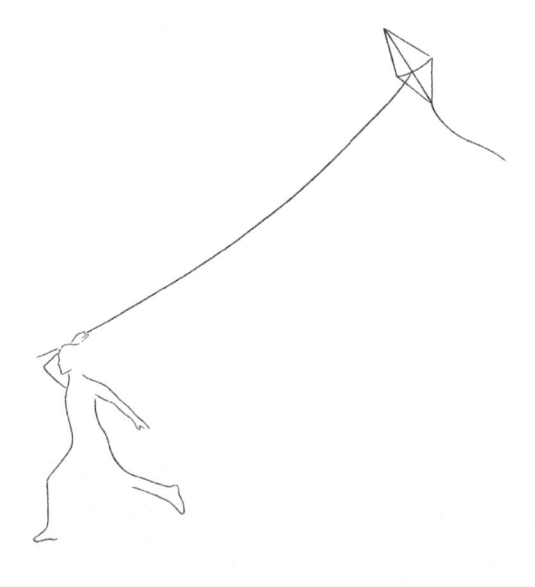

You're amazing in every way :)

Q&A 1

"Plz do a video about finding a hobby I've been really struggling with finding my passion."

Struggling to find a hobby or what you love can feel frustrating.

Sometimes what your family and friends say can have an impact on you.

The fear of their judgement can get in the way.

This might stop you from owning what you love and what you're passionate about.

So ask yourself:

"If I knew no one could judge me, what would I do?"

"If everyone I knew supported me, what would I love to do?"

And keep exploring different things.

Don't be afraid of making mistakes.

You have a whole life ahead of you to find out what you love.

This life is one big game to play.

A playground to explore.

And you don't have to be good at your passion.

Don't put pressure on yourself.

All that matters is that it brings you joy and happiness.

You loving it, often leads to you being good at it as well.

So don't worry and enjoy exploring.

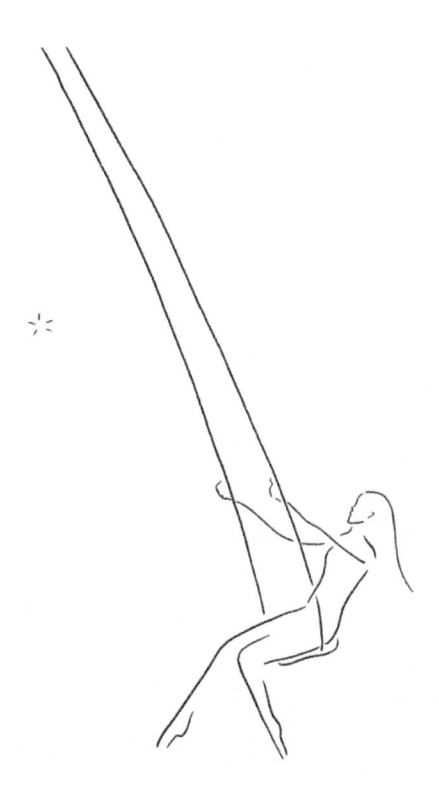

You're amazing in every way :)

Q&A 2

"Every time I mention it, my family and friends just break out in laughter. What should I do? Like it's my dream."

Don't seek validation for your dreams.

If your friends and family are laughing at your dreams, let them laugh.

They're your dreams.

They're not their dreams.

They don't have to understand it.

No one will see it and understand it the way you do.

It makes sense for you, because it's yours.

It's ok if they don't get it.

Don't share your dreams with those who you know will laugh.

Your dreams are sacred and need to be honoured.

Only share with those who will get it and will support you.

Keep pouring love and energy into your dreams.

They will get it once you create it.

Then they're going to celebrate with you.

You don't have to prove your dreams to anyone.

They're yours.

So don't worry about what they say and keep going.

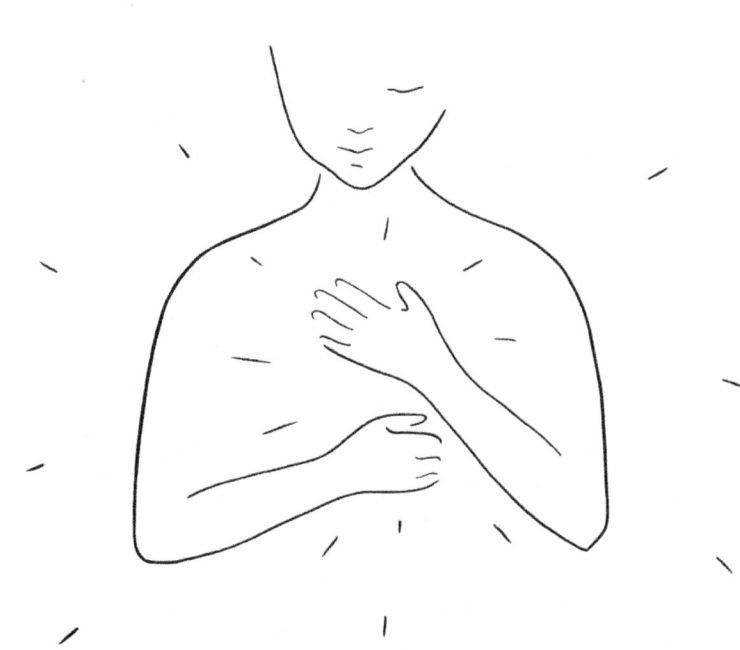

You're amazing in every way :)

Q&A 3

"What if people stop you from following your dream?"

People might be stopping you from following your dream.

This is because you believe they can.

You're a powerful creator and you create your own reality.

Shift your focus from believing others have the power to stop you to believing you have the power to create what you want.

Others only have power if you give it to them.

You're amazing in every way :)

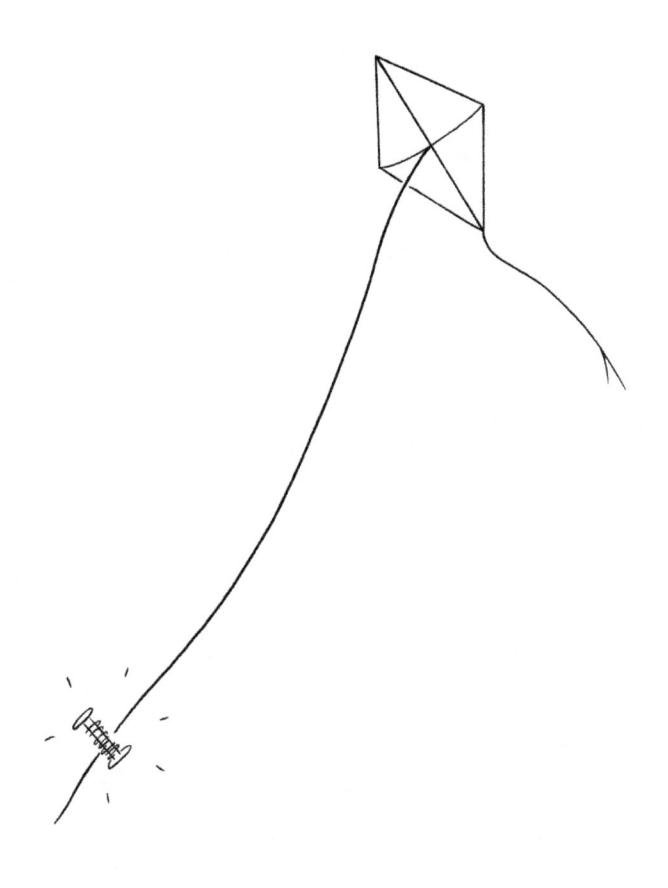

WOMANHOOD

Part 132 - You're Becoming A Woman

You're not a child anymore.

You're entering adulthood.

Your body will be going through changes.

It will start to produce hormones for your sexual development.

Your boobs might hurt.

You might not be able to sleep on your front for a while.

You might grow so tall all of a sudden.

You might be clumsy for a while and feel unbalanced.

You might feel ugly.

You might have mood swings.

You will have your period.

You might feel more impulsive.

You might have spots on your face.

Your hormones might even affect the way you think about dating.

Be patient with the changes in your body.

This is a time of change and growth.

And it will pass.

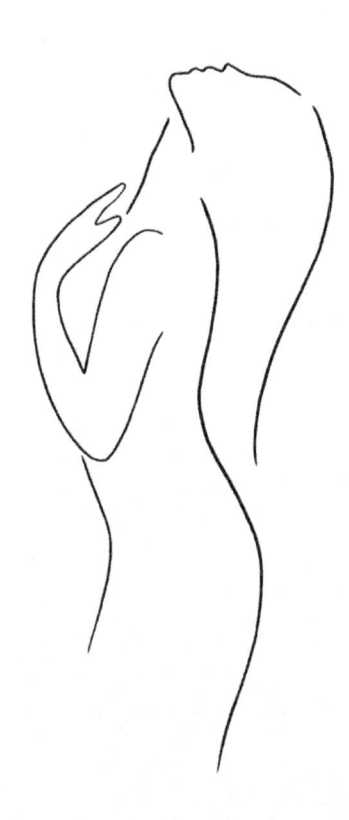

You're amazing in every way :)

Part 133 - Your Body Is A Miracle

Your body is a miracle.

You're breathing without thinking about it.

Your heart is beating without stopping.

You're digesting everything you eat.

You're constantly regenerating your cells.

If you hurt yourself physically, your body heals itself.

You have your menstrual cycle that actually creates life.

It's pretty amazing what your body is doing for you.

What is there not to love about your body?

It loves you no matter how you treat it.

It keeps you alive.

Don't just focus on how your body looks.

Focus on how you feel in your body.

Appreciate your body.

Appreciate all the things your body does for you.

You're amazing in every way :)

Part 134 - Love Your Body

Love your body.

To love your body on all levels, you have to go beyond the physical.

Go beyond what you see.

What you see on social media is loving the body on a physical level.

We're only seeing beautiful bodies from the outside.

Loving your body is something that comes from the inside.

Your body is your vessel that nourishes and feeds you.

It allows you to live and enjoy life.

You can dance.

You can walk and jump

You can taste incredible food.

You can listen to music.

You can experience pleasure all through your body.

Sunshine on your face.

A hot bath.

A lovely massage.

A hug from someone you love.

What you can experience, thanks to your body, is endless.

Here's how you can love your body more:

Get naked and stand in front of the mirror.

Look at your body.

Go through every part of your body, from your head to your feet.

Place your hand on the body part and say,

"I'm sorry."

"I love you."

Do this especially with body parts you might not like.

You might have negative thoughts come up as you do this.

Let them dissolve away.

Saying "I'm sorry" is to apologise for all the times you didn't treat your body with love and respect.

Or for when you might have allowed such behaviour from others.

And that's ok.

It's never too late to say sorry and forgive yourself.

Saying "I love you" is to pour love into that part of the body.

You deserve this.

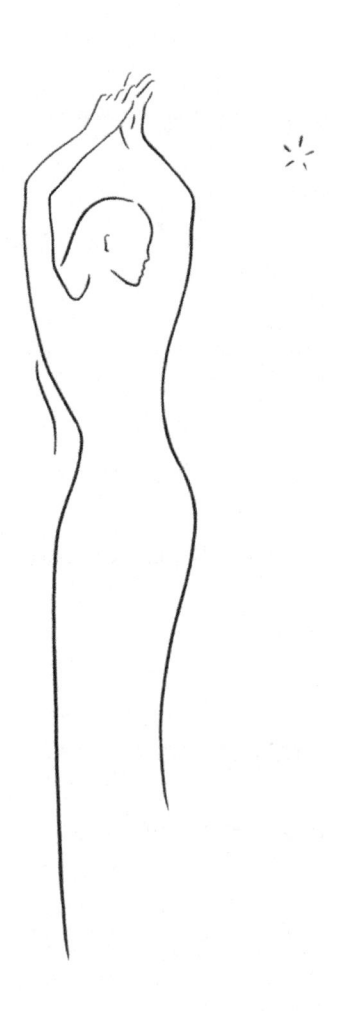

You're amazing in every way :)

Part 135 - You're Beautiful

True beauty shines from the inside out.

You're beautiful when you're being yourself.

You're beautiful when you're loving.

You're beautiful when you're doing something that lights you up and something that you're passionate about.

You're beautiful as you are.

Your body is beautiful as it is.

Imagine looking at your face in the mirror.

See yourself through the eyes of love.

How would love see your face?

See the beauty your body has.

Don't let the people you surround yourself with define your definition of beauty.

You get to define what is beautiful to you.

It comes solely from yourself.

The beauty standards you see on social media are not real.

It comes from plastic surgery, filters or photoshop.

They're not naturally attainable.

So when you sit there and compare yourself with these models, you're comparing yourself with something that's not real.

You're dismissing your uniqueness.

Don't do that to yourself.

See how unique you are.

There is no one quite like you.

And that is beautiful.

You're amazing in every way :)

Part 136 - Make-Up

Your face is beautiful without make-up.

Make-up only enhances the beauty you already have.

You don't have to wear it every day.

Ever since I was fourteen, I wore make-up every day up until a few years ago.

I didn't wear make-up for a whole year. It was hard but also very freeing. Now I wear it when I want to.

Use make-up to adorn yourself.

To express your creativity and for fun.

Not to cover up.

You're amazing in every way :)

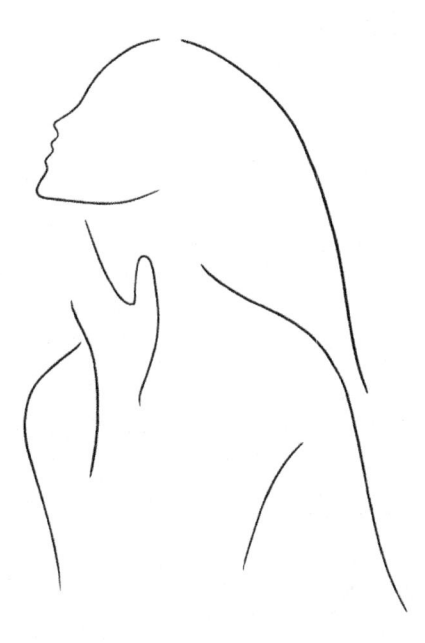

Part 137 - Sisterhood

Other girls are not your enemies.

They're your sisters.

Look out for them.

Protect them.

Love them.

There is no comparison.

Don't try to get their boy behind their back.

Celebrate them when something great happens in their lives.

Know that there's more where it came from.

It's an abundant universe.

Their win isn't your loss.

Their win is your win.

When one sister wins, we all win.

You're amazing in every way :)

Part 138 - Periods

When you start to go through bodily changes, you will have your period.

There's nothing shameful about having periods.

Thanks to your period, you can create life.

This is something to celebrate.

Your period is part of your menstrual cycle.

Your menstrual cycle has winter, spring, summer, autumn in one month.

Just like there are four seasons in one year, your body also goes through four seasons in one month.

If you live in alignment with this, you will feel much more connected to yourself and your body.

Winter is when you have your period.

This lasts between 3-7 days.

Just like winter, this is the time to hibernate to go inwards and to be still.

Allow yourself to be with yourself at least one day.

Try to reduce contact with the outside world as much as you can.

You're meant to rest when you have your period.

You can even change your bed sheets to a red set of sheets to honour this time.*

And give yourself some rest.

Spring comes after your period is over.

During spring, life starts to come back in nature.

Your energy will start to rise.

This is a great time to make some plans and start new habits.

You will have more willpower during this time.

This phase could last up to a week.

Then comes the summer.

This is when you ovulate.

You're in full bloom.

You might feel more outgoing during this time.

Your confidence might be higher.

This is a great time to be social and to have important conversations or events lined up.

After summer comes autumn.

Just like the leaves falling down in autumn, this is a great time to let go.

Emotionally, energetically, mentally and physically.

It's a great time to declutter.

This is when your energy levels start to drop.

You might also start to feel more inwards, wanting alone time.

This time also tells you what needs to change in your life.

So listen to your body and what it's saying.

During this time, you might feel extra emotional and sensitive.

So don't be hard on yourself and be extra kind to yourself.

This premenstrual time lasts between one or two weeks before your period.

Then it's winter again where you have your period.

The more you allow yourself to rest in winter, the higher energy you'll have during your summer.

Track your period. Plan your life around it.

As women, we are cyclical beings.

When you work with your cycle, your whole life will change.

You're amazing in every way :)

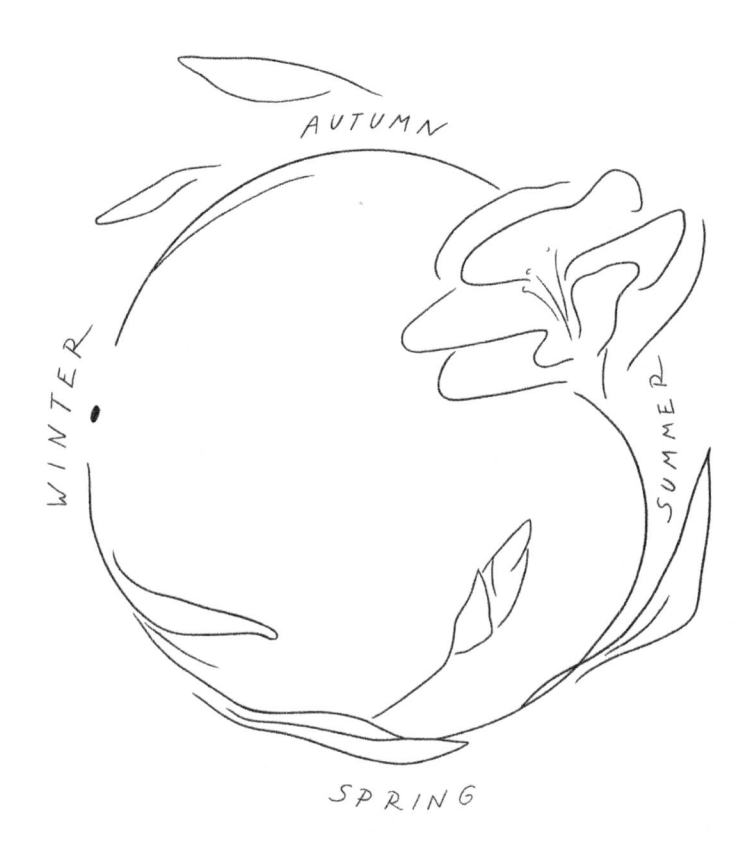

*I learnt how to live in alignment with my cycle including this tip from my friend Claire Baker who is the author of *50 Things You Need To Know About Periods.*

Part 139 - Enjoy Your Attractions

As you grow through life, you will have different attractions.

Don't judge yourself for what you're attracted to.

Approach your attractions with curiosity.

Let them show you a part of you.

Let them teach you.

Let them heal you.

Allow yourself to grow from them.

It's all one big journey.

Enjoy the journey.

You're amazing in every way :)

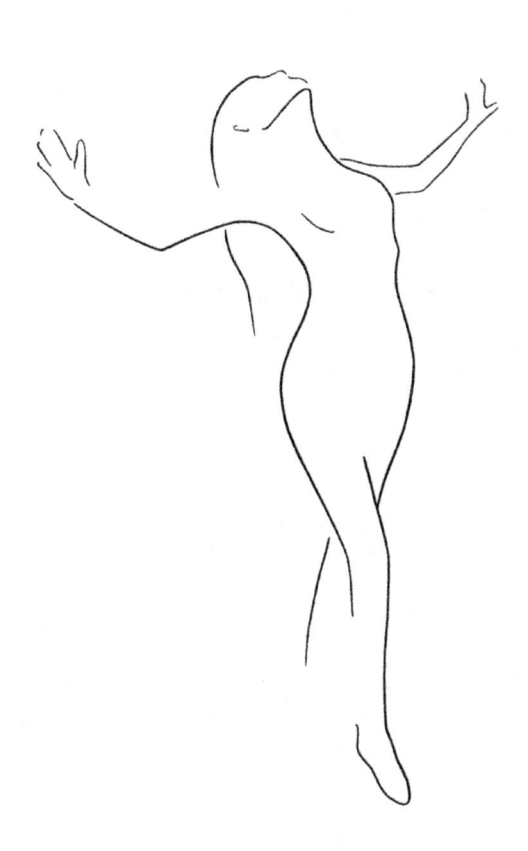

Part 140 - Don't Rush Into Sex

Don't rush into sex.

Don't feel pressured into it.

My mum used to tell me that when I was younger,

"Your body will be ready for sex, but your Soul might not be ready. Wait until your Soul is ready too."

I was 19 when I had sex for the first time.

He was a good friend from high school.

After I went to university, we dated.

I felt safe with him and trusted him.

I felt loved and respected by him.

It felt right for my first time to be with him.

He's still a good friend of mine and I love him dearly.

So take your time.

There's no rush.

You're not missing out on anything.

You're amazing in every way :)

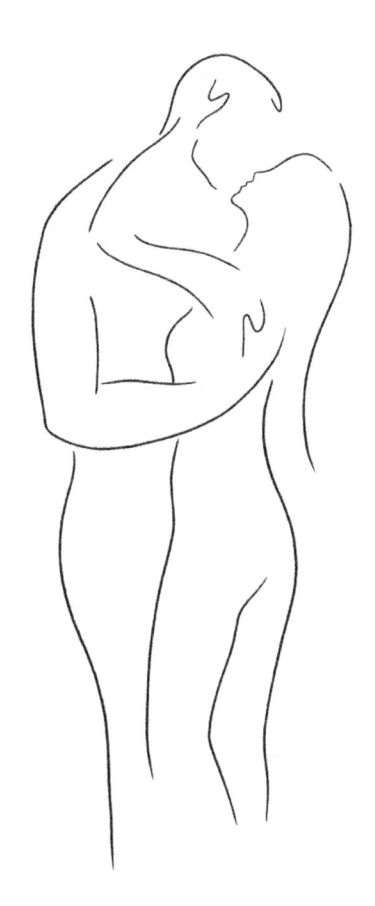

DISCLAIMER:

You should always feel safe with whom you're sharing emotional or physical intimacy.

Here's a link to age of consent around the world to be informed:

https://www.ageofconsent.net/world

Q&A 1

"I was wondering if you could do a video on if you were 14 and possibly starting to question your sexuality a lil' bit."

It is very natural to question your sexuality when you're 14.

We're complex beings.

We're not black and white.

We have so many parts of us.

Your sexuality is yours to explore.

Take your time to find out who you are and what you desire.

You're amazing in every way :)

Q&A 2

"So this might be an unusual one but I have already lost my virginity at 16 and boys are making me feel less worthy because of it. Any advice?"

No one has the right to judge you for your decisions.

What you decide to do with your body is up to you.

This is your life.

You get to decide what you want.

You don't have to buy into what boys are saying.

Love and accept yourself for who you are.

And for the decisions that you've made in the past.

It's all ok.

Know that you're incredibly worthy.

You're incredibly loveable.

You're amazing in every way :)

Q&A 3

"I know this might be weird but my face is really not symmetrical, and I think I look different in the mirror than to what others see me as."

Your face is not meant to be symmetrical.

Maybe you saw this from the filters on social media.

In real life, most people's faces are not symmetrical.

You can Google "symmetrical faces" and see how weird it looks.

My face isn't symmetrical either.

My eyebrows are never the same.

My smile is different from different sides.

Because I'm human.

So are you.

Love your face as it is.

It's unique and beautiful.

You're amazing in every way :)

NOW WHAT?

Now go and create an amazing life for yourself!

Come back to this book from time to time.

If this book touched your heart, give it as a gift to a friend.

If you want me to come and talk at your school, ask your teacher.

Have them email me on isik@isiktlabar.com with the subject "Talk in School".

Follow me on @isiktlabar on Instagram and TikTok.

Thank you for going on this journey with me!

I hope to meet with you again :)

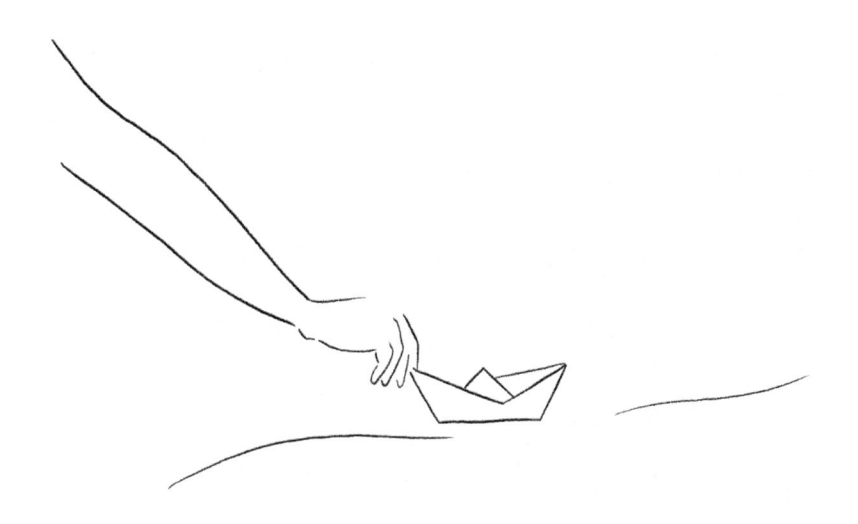

WHAT WAS I LIKE WHEN I WAS 14?

"Can you tell us about your 14 year old self?"

I was incredibly shy.

I was very self-conscious and insecure.

When I walked, I didn't know what to do with my arms or where to put my hands.

I had a lot of shame about myself.

I just wanted to disappear and for people to not look at me.

I really cared about what boys thought of me.

I gave my worth and power away to boys a lot.

My worth depended on how much someone liked me.

I didn't have a good relationship with my parents.

I didn't want to be around them much.

I was very rebellious and stubborn in my own way.

I'm an only child. I don't have any brothers or sisters.

I felt very lonely and misunderstood.

I had a cat. I spent a lot of time with my cat and my friends.

At times, I loved life.

At times, I didn't want to exist.

And I didn't know exactly what I wanted to do when I grew up.

I felt all this pressure that I had to know.

So that's how I was when I was 14.

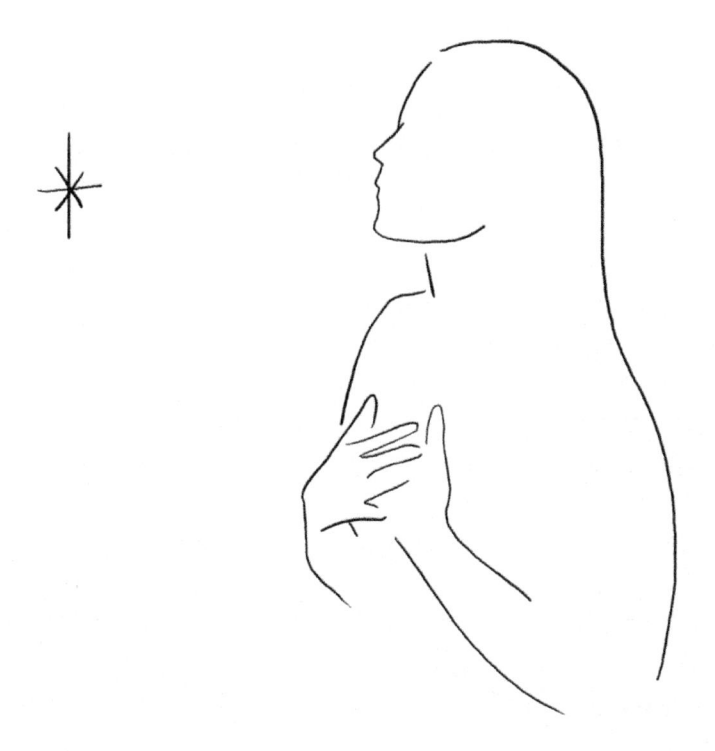

HOW DID I BECOME WHO I AM NOW?

"When did you start becoming who you are now? And did you make the change or did it just happen? Ily"

It didn't happen overnight.

Since I was 14, I've been into personal growth, psychology and spirituality.

I read books and attended many courses.

I worked on myself a lot.

I discovered who I am and how I want to live my life.

As I write this, I'm 32.

So that's 18 years of going deep into myself, uncovering what's in me and sharing that with the world.

The biggest thing that helped me was that every time I learnt something, I applied it.

No matter how small it was, I took action on it.

I shared it with my friends as if I was teaching them.

I used to be very shy.

So I would put myself in situations where I would go and talk to people even when I didn't feel like it.

Still to this day, I always ask myself:

"What do I want?"

"What would I love?"

Following the answer naturally helps me become more of who I truly am.

So I would say keep learning.

Keep growing.

Keep exploring.

And keep taking action towards your truth.

WHAT I STUDIED & WHAT I DO NOW

"Heyy! I have a question: What did you study and what job do you have? Cause I saw in one of your tiktoks saying that you were interested in psychology."

I studied architecture.

During my studies, I realised it wasn't what I wanted to do.

I felt like a bird trying to swim underwater.

It felt very unnatural.

After graduating, I gave myself permission to go and create my own business.

I'm an intuition coach and breathwork facilitator.

Now I've been running my own business for seven years guiding people to live their highest potential and to be themselves in the world.

I help them heal and create their dreams.

What I do has nothing to do with what I studied.

I was always into personal development, psychology and spirituality.

I just turned that into my full time job.

And I love it!

It gives me so much joy seeing people being themselves in the world and following their joy.

It was my dream to do this.

And I'm doing it.

You too can create your own dream.

BOOKS

Here are the powerful books that impacted my life in the last 15 years.

Throughout the book, there were references to some of them:

Calling in "The One" - Katherine Woodward Thomas

Cry, Heart, But Never Break - Ringtved / Pardi

Daisy Ella's Sparkle Search - Lauren Sarfas

Eleven Minutes - Paulo Coelho

Good Night Stories for Rebel Girls - Elena Favilli

Jonathan Livingston Seagull - Richard Bach

Living, Loving and Learning - Leo Buscaglia

Manual of the Warrior of Light - Paulo Coelho

Maps to Ecstasy - Gabrielle Roth

Medicine Dance - Marsha Scarbrough

Part's Work - Tom Holmes

Shift Your Mind Shift The World - Steve Chandler

Tao Te Ching - Lao Tzu - Stephen Mitchell

The Alchemist - Paulo Coelho

The Artist's Way - Julia Cameron

The Illusion of Money - Kyle Cease

The Little Prince - Antoine de Saint-Exupery

The Magician's Way - William Whitecloud

The Secrets of Natural Success - William Whitecloud

The Shaman's Last Apprentice - Rebekah Shaman

The Wisdom of the Enneagram - Don Richard Riso and Russ Hudson

Unbound - Kasia Urbaniak

Untamed - Glennon Doyle

War of Art - Steven Pressfield

100 Ways To Motivate Yourself - Steven Chandler

50 Things You Need To Know About Periods - Claire Baker

ABOUT THE AUTHOR

Isik Tlabar is an intuition coach and a breathwork facilitator.

She has 18 years of experience of personal and spiritual development - psychology, creative development, shadow and energy work, alchemy, shamanic practices, sacred sexuality, breathwork and conscious dance practices.

She has worked with hundreds of people connecting them with their essence so they can live their highest potential.

Isik has led workshops, retreats and online programs for deeper self-actualization as well as breathwork and dance journeys at the Mind, Body & Spirit Festival, How The Light Gets In and Latitude Festival in the UK.

This is her first book.

You can follow her @isiktlabar on Instagram and TikTok and get in touch through www.isiktlabar.com

ABOUT THE ILLUSTRATOR

Irem Kale is a creative consultant specialising in branding, particularly within the hospitality industry.

She sculpts brand identities and crafts individual personas while ensuring an integration of different elements to create memorable luxury experiences.

Irem received her bachelor's degree in architecture at Politecnico di Milano.

Her creative expertise, encompassing many mediums and thrives in the convergence of diverse cultures.

This is her first time illustrating.

You can check her work and get in touch through www.iremkale.it

Printed in Great Britain
by Amazon